A Journey in Search of Ancestors

The English Cotswolds to the Wairarapa in New Zealand

CHRISTOPHER POPE

FRASER BOOKS

To Kathy
My constant companion on this journey.

Published by Fraser Books,
Chamberlain Road, RD8, Masterton, New Zealand
First published December 2008

ISBN: 978-0-9582988-0-3

Formatting: Christine Miller, Printcraft, Masterton
Printed by Printcraft '81 Ltd, 289 Queen Street, Masterton 5810

Front cover: the 1890 Committee of the Masterton A & P Association.
Augustus Cave, second from left, front row.
Back cover: the Cave family crest on a plaque at Richmond Palace.
© Peter Denton

CONTENTS

PREFACE

This is a very personal account of my searches into my family's history and genealogy. These searches have taken me into churchyards, libraries, county record offices, national archives, and museums in England and New Zealand. My wife Kathy has been my ever-present companion and supporter and together we have discovered exciting information about my family history. These facts have given me a greater understanding of the past and, in particular, of my family.

I was born in Bristol, England, on April 29 1939 and was educated from 1946-56 at the local grammar school, where history was my favourite subject. I studied accountancy for five years and after qualifying, I set up my own practice. In 1966 I married Kathleen White, a nursing sister who later became the hospital manager of the Plymouth Nuffield Hospital, the largest provider of private healthcare in the south-west of England, and part of Nuffield Hospitals.

My father, Arthur Herbert Pope, was a foreign travel enthusiast. He organised each year in the 1950s superb holidays for groups of about 35 people, mainly from his own workplace, to go to exciting destinations in Europe. At this time, so soon after the end of the Second World War, there were very few travel companies selling foreign holidays, so his organised tours were always very popular and well supported. My mother and I went with him all over Europe for 10 consecutive years and we had many interesting and unusual adventures – and indeed some amusing mishaps! So successful were these trips that four people, who met for the first time on my father's tours, later married.

These holidays, affectionately known as 'Pope's Tours', gave me the taste for foreign travel. I was able to combine two of my main interests, namely history and travel. Little did I realise when I started tracing my family tree, this would lead me to the other side of the world. However, my foreign travel adventures were insignificant in comparison with those of my forefathers, Augustus William Cave and his father, William Cave, who must have endured considerable hardship and danger on their long sea voyages to New Zealand in the 19th century.

I discovered many interesting facts about the lives of Augustus and William. Augustus was one of the early pioneers of the town of Masterton, North Island, New Zealand, and I was proud to learn he became a highly respected member of the local community. He was connected by marriage to the Masters, Iorns, Bannister and Perry families, who were some of the most influential people in the founding and development of the town. Augustus had strong ties with the local Maori community who held him in such high esteem that they presented him with a flax-woven waistcoat.

Probably the most exciting discovery, because I am an only child and have no close relatives in England, was that I had second cousins in another country. Also, as I have been gradually uncovering facts about the lives of Augustus, his wife, and his father in New Zealand, I have met some wonderful people who have now become good friends and I have visited many splendid places.

Recently, my friend Bob Russell and I also discovered another of my cousins was Viscount Cave, who became Home Secretary in the First World War and Lord Chancellor of Great Britain in 1922. He also became Chancellor of the University of Oxford and was awarded the GCMG.

Tracing one's ancestors can be fun, fascinating, full of drama and very rewarding. My experience in tracing one branch of my family tree over the last 15 years has been all of these things and more.

I was determined to write this book, not only because I am proud of Augustus and his father, and of Viscount Cave, but because I hoped other people might be encouraged by my own good luck to start researching their own family trees. All I can say is that it is a journey well worth travelling. So many of us have fascinating forebears, and it just needs time and patience to discover them. Good luck with your family researching!

Christopher Pope
October 2008.

ACKNOWLEDGEMENTS

Many people have helped me in my researches of the Cave family tree, but a special mention should be made of the following for their specific help.

Bob Russell inspired me to start tracing my family tree and provided his invaluable help in uncovering my family secrets in England before I started my researches in New Zealand.

Gareth Winter, the Masterton archivist, with his vast knowledge of the history of the Wairarapa, gave me much information about Augustus William Cave and his enthusiasm for his work encouraged me to embark on this project.

Margaret Thomas, Edyth Herrington, Barbara Nichols, Beryl and Neil Stuart, my newly discovered relatives, supplied me with many photographs, documents and newspaper cuttings. Best of all, they recounted to me many interesting stories about Augustus and his wife Mary Ann. Sadly, Neil Stuart and Edyth Herrington have now died, so I'm sorry they cannot see the results of their contributions.

Also, I am most grateful to Tom and Andrea Wyeth for all their help in organising the gift of a bell to the Te Ore Ore marae.

Piri Te Tau and Jim Rimene from the Te Ore Ore marae kindly lent me a superb photograph of the Maori chief Wi Tinitara Te Kaewa, from whom Augustus purchased land in 1872.

I should also like to thank for their help Betty Rewi, of Te Papa Museum, Graham Southey of the A & P Association, the late Richard Hall of Gawith Burridge and the late Angus McCallum, author of *A Meeting of Gentlemen on Matters Agricultural.* The staff at the Wairarapa Archive, the Masterton Library, the Masterton District Council, the *Wairarapa Times Age* and the Wellington Land Registry were all very courteous and eager to assist me in my quest for information about my relatives and the early years of Masterton.

Our farm stay hosts, Elaine and Arthur Dew of Pokohiwi Road and Glenys Hansen of Cootes Road, Matahiwi, drove my wife and me to various places for my researches. They also did some useful word processing, particularly of the wills of my relatives, and they even held dinner parties for us and the various people I had met in the local area during my investigations. Both families were enthusiastic about the project and practically everyone I came into contact with during my researches was keen to help and learn more about the beginnings of Masterton. I feel there is still a pioneering spirit about the people of New Zealand; their country is young and there is a keenness to learn about their past.

I should also like to thank the editor of the *Wairarapa Times Age* for publishing two splendid articles written by Gareth and Owen Winter about my researches and my visits to Masterton.

Also my thanks go to Pani Himona from the Te Ore Ore marae for organising the welcome (powhiri) for me and all my guests – it was a very moving experience.

My gratitude goes to the editor of the *Wairarapa News* for publishing an article by Piers Fuller regarding the gift of the bell: "Ancestral quest comes full circle at Te Ore Ore".

I should also like to thank Lord Faulkner of Worcester for showing me my family's coat of arms mounted on a wall in a corridor in the House of Lords, and the painting of Lord Cave as Lord Chancellor sitting in the River Room. Also my thanks must go to Emma Gormley at the Palace of Westminster and to Dr. Anthony Boyce of St. John's College for helping to organise the photographic reproduction of the paintings of Lord Cave in the River Room of the House of Lords and as Chancellor of Oxford University.

There are many more people – too numerous to mention – who helped me in my researches and my thanks go out to all of them for the kindness shown to Kathy and me.

Finally, I should like to pay tribute to my dear friends, Pat Hewertson, Ross Greig, Keith White, Nonnie and Alan Duncan and Simon Dorset who assisted me with editorial work on the book, to Ian Blair – the present owner of 'Field Farm', my family's former farm – for his help, and my wife Kathy for all her patience and good humour while I spent so many hours on my researches and preparing this book.

C P

Wedding photograph of Christopher Pope's grandparents in 1897. Front row: second left, his grandfather Herbert George Fleming, then his grandmother Kate Insall and Mary Elizabeth Insall (née Cave) Augustus Cave's sister and Christopher Pope's great-grandmother. Back row: far right, John Insall Christopher Pope's great-grandfather.

CHAPTER 1

A JOURNEY BACK IN TIME

It all began in 1990 at a Pope family dinner party when the subject of genealogy was brought up by Bob Russell, a colleague of my wife at Nuffield Hospitals, a group of private hospitals based in the UK. I am sure many interesting subjects besides politics, religion and the British weather are discussed daily over the dinner tables around the country but this evening's subject proved to be particularly fascinating.

Bob related how he had traced a branch of his family back to Ireland and that one of his ancestors had been a justice of the King's Bench in Ireland. The judge, Godfrey Boate, was immortalised by Jonathan Swift, the great Irish writer and cleric. He went on to say he had spent many years delving into his family history and had managed, with some persistence and much patience, to trace this branch back to the 15th century.

Our dinner guests were amazed Bob had managed to get so far back. There were questions about how one could research one's own family tree. From 1837, according to Bob, it was a relatively straightforward task using public records in England and Wales. However, it could be more difficult if a very common surname, such as Smith or Jones, was being searched. He then went on to say that by making two or three visits to St. Catherine's House in Aldwych , London, much genealogical information could be gathered. The central civil registrars of births, marriages and deaths in England and Wales from the third quarter of 1837 are kept there.

Bob also mentioned his family researches had led him to many places where he had met very interesting people and, best of all, had discovered intriguing facts about his ancestors. All our guests were fired with enthusiasm and we talked well into the night about unusual happenings to the relatives we were acquainted with.

I loved history at school and, having passed 'A' level 'European History from 1660 to 1815', I suppose it was inevitable I should not only become involved in the history of my family but also enjoy every minute of my research.

A few weeks later, when my wife Kathy and I were up in London on business, I decided to spend a few hours at St. Catherine's House. Amazingly, on this first visit, I discovered eight vital dates relating to my family tree. When the certificates arrived a few weeks later, I learned a great deal more about my ancestors which was completely unknown to me. Over the next six months, buoyed up by my discoveries, I visited St. Catherine's House a further four times and on each occasion found more key dates for my family tree. These dates produced more certificates, and, having studied all the information I had amassed, I found I had details of 15 of my 16 great-great-grandparents! I remembered Bob Russell telling me that if one can trace 13 of your great-great-grandparents you have done well! The occupations of the males in my family tree conjured up pictures of a different age. Adam Butt was "a stationery engine driver", Henry Fleming "a master basket maker", Hartland Roe "a shoemaker", Thomas Insall "a horse dealer" and William Cave "a yeoman". Perhaps one day my descendants will be just as intrigued by Christopher Paul Pope "an accountant".

It was now necessary to decide where to concentrate my efforts. My maternal grandfather, Herbert George Fleming, who lived with us in Bristol for many years, told me when I was a small boy that his ancestors were Scottish and belonged to the Murray of Atholl clan who hailed from Perth. Grandfather Fleming also said the laird of the clan and his brothers fought for Bonnie Prince Charlie. Their castle was sacked by the English and all perished apart from one young brother, Herbert's ancestor. The authenticity of this story has not been confirmed to date. It was a great shame I did not question my grandfather further, but as a young schoolboy I was largely preoccupied collecting train numbers. On one of my rare visits to London with my grandfather he asked me where I wanted to go. Of course, I chose King's Cross station so I could collect train numbers of the LNER railway. As I lived in Bristol, I could only collect numbers of GWR trains, so it was a real treat for me to go to a different region.

The only other branch of the family I knew something about was the Cave family on my mother's side. Both my mother, Vera Mary Pope, (née Fleming) and her sister Florence Muriel Wilkins told me there was a 'Cave' farmhouse in the Cotswolds which my grandmother, Kate Fleming, (née Insall) had visited. It was called 'Field Farm' and was situated on the outskirts of a village called Nympsfield. They also told me they had a cousin named Richard Eric Cave Insall. He was a bachelor who had lived all his life in the same house in Bishopston, a district of Bristol. His father, Robert Insall, was the brother of my grandmother, Kate Fleming, and their father, John Insall, had married Mary Elizabeth Cave in 1864. Eric was a family history enthusiast and one day in 1995 my mother invited him for afternoon tea. He was a lovely old gentleman and I learned a great deal from him about the Caves.

Although I would have liked to explore the Pope family history first, I decided it would be easier to start my research on the Cave side, as the Cotswolds were the handiest to visit. The Caves were farmers and, as farmers tended to stay put in one area, this was another factor influencing the decision and would help my research through the census returns.

With great excitement, I set off one sunny June day to the village of Nympsfield. A couple of days earlier I had looked up the origins of Nympsfield and was interested to note that, unlike most Gloucestershire parishes which date back to Anglo-Saxon times, Nympsfield appears to be much older. The name comes from a Celtic word 'nymed' meaning a sacred grove. Such sites were used by the Druids and here it probably refers to West Hill. The shape of the parish boundaries also says much: Nympsfield sits square and secure on the high ground while its neighbours seem to be reaching out to grasp a small parcel of the sacred high ground.

I had already pinpointed 'Field Farm' on the map but had no idea if the farmhouse was still standing. I arrived in Nympsfield about midday and decided to have lunch at the local pub. You can imagine my surprise when entering the bar, I found the census return for 1891 hanging on the wall with 'Field Farm' and its occupants clearly mentioned. I asked the landlord if he knew whether 'Field Farm' still existed and, if so, who owned the property and who was living there. To my relief and excitement, he said 'Field Farm' was still standing with a Mr Blair the current owner and occupier. I telephoned Mr Ian Blair from the pub and he immediately invited me to visit him.

When I arrived Ian showed me around the ground floor and then the barns and outhouses. He kept horses which was a pleasant surprise as I knew that, in the past, the Caves had been breeders of horses. He also showed me two old pennies dated 1803 and 1804 which had been found in the roof. Since the farmhouse had been built around the turn of the 19th century, it would be nice to think they were dropped by the original builders. It was a lovely old farmhouse; well built with an attractive overhanging roof, which Ian informed me had been a new architectural idea at the time.

After my visit to 'Field Farm', I made my way to the lovely old church at Uley. I asked a man tidying up the grounds if he had ever heard of the Caves. To my complete surprise, he replied that the Cave family was well known and I should look into the 'Bread Charity' the Cave family had helped to set up a couple of centuries ago. I immediately made my way to the vicarage at the Nympsfield church. The vicar

'Field Farm', Nympsfield.

very kindly lent me the keys to the vestry, where I found in an extremely old deed box, the document setting up the Bread Charity. It was called the 'Nympsfield Club'. It had been set up for the poor of Nympsfield and the deed had been signed by Thomas Cave, Church Warden.

It was now getting late, so I thanked the vicar for his help and made my way back to Bristol with a real sense of achievement. To find the farm still standing was a bonus but to discover the Bread Charity and its origins was an exceptional find. This had certainly been a great day as far as research into my family history was concerned.

Several months later I returned to London to complete the missing dates on my chart detailing all the descendants of my great-great- grandfathers. I was particularly anxious to fill in all the dates regarding the Cave side of the family. But in the end I was left with one date I could not find. I could not trace the death certificate of my great-great-grandfather William Cave. His birth date was June 14 1807 and he was married on May 24 1838, but I simply could not find the date when he died. The death indexes are listed in very large bound volumes, each one covering a quarter of a year. I started with the first volume in 1838 (3rd quarter) and continued right up to 1917 (when he would have been aged 110!) but I could not find any trace of his death. I thought I might have missed the entry, so I went through every volume again without success. It was a complete mystery and I left St. Catherine's House that evening very deflated and absolutely exhausted.

CHAPTER 2

A PILGRIMAGE

I asked Bob Russell for advice about how to track down
William Cave's death certificate. Bob suggested I return to
Nympsfield and search through the graveyard of the local
church. It was several months before I was able to do so,
but when I did I was thrilled to find the churchyard had a
special section for the Cave family. Here I discovered several
Cave box tombs and on one of these was the following
inscription:

> Mary, w/o Thomas CAVE of this parish,
> 29 April 1798, 57
> also two of their children
> Mary Ann, Feb 1790 - 17 May 1800
> John, 26 June 1797 - 15 May 1800
> Caroline, w/o William CAVE, 20 Oct 1879, 59
> William CAVE, 16 Dec 1897, and died at
> Woodleigh Masterton, New Zealand, aged 95

That solved the problem of the death certificate.
Obviously, this would have been issued in New Zealand.
But for me, this was an amazing discovery and, definitely,

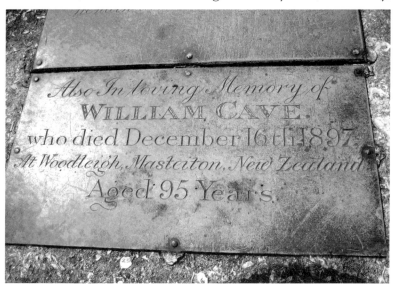

*Inscription, Nympsfield
church.*

Graveyard, Nympsfield church.

a eureka moment. Naturally, I was intrigued to know why he went to the other side of the world, how he got there, and at what age he went.

I checked the 1881 Census and found that William Cave was then a widower, aged about 72 years. He was still farming 'Field Farm'. (He was actually 74 because I discovered he was baptised at Nympsfield on June 14 1807.) By 1891, William was no longer in England as there was no record of him in the 1891 Census for England. Therefore, he must have gone to New Zealand sometime between 1881 and 1891.

For a man, far older than the life expectancy for a male at that time, to undertake such a hazardous journey was truly remarkable, but this is exactly what William Cave did. In the 1880s any journey to New Zealand by sailing ship took several months and was fraught with danger and disease. When Henry Jones, an earlier Masterton pioneer, sailed to the colony in 1842 it was reported that 19 people had died on the voyage, among them his youngest child.

A few years later, when I was planning a five month round-the-world trip to celebrate our 30th wedding anniversary, I decided to earmark two days for a visit to Masterton in New Zealand to see if I could possibly unravel the mystery of why William Cave had set out on such a dangerous voyage in his seventies.

At last, in October 1996, it was time for our lengthy trip and Kathy and I set off for New Zealand via short stays in

Hong Kong, Bangkok and Singapore. Nine months earlier we had organised, through a company named Worldwide Home Exchange Club to swap our house in Devon and our car for a month with the Hilton family in Devonport, New Zealand. They came to our house in June 1996 and later told us they had a wonderfully restful holiday. They were at Auckland airport to meet us and then drove us to their home at Devonport. After we had settled in, they left and we arranged to meet up again at a hotel near Auckland airport in a month's time.

Devonport is a lovely old colonial style village, with a ferry running direct to the centre of Auckland every 15 minutes. We spent a delightful fortnight exploring the local area with a trip to the Bay of Islands, and we then set off to journey south to Masterton.

First, we visited the Coromandel Peninsula, a very beautiful part of the country with a rugged coastline, and then journeyed to Rotorua. Here steam and hot air bubble out of the ground all over the place and, so I am told, the local hospital has piped itself into the ground and consequently has a constant source of free hot water! It is a simply amazing town which one has to visit to fully appreciate.

We duly arrived in Masterton on a hot summer's day at the beginning of December 1996 and from that moment onwards our feet hardly touched the ground. In fact we stayed six days but in the end time ran out and we had to leave to drive 450 miles in one day to Auckland to catch the plane to Australia early the next day from where we were to continue our round the world trip.

The first port of call in Masterton was the local burial ground. When I mentioned the name 'Cave' in the cemetery office, I was immediately told to look in the Pioneer Section of the cemetery. My heart started to race and in a short while I found the family grave, which immediately answered a number of my questions. The gravestone mentioned my great-great-grandfather William Cave but also his eldest son, Augustus William Cave and his wife Mary Ann and their son, William Henry who, sadly, had died at the age of six. This information answered my burning question of why my great-great-grandfather had come to New Zealand so late in his life. His wife, Caroline Cave, my great-great-grandmother, had died in 1879 so he had come to New Zealand to spend the rest of his life with his eldest son whom he had not seen for many years. Augustus had left England at the age of 22 in 1862.

I then called at the Masterton tourist office where, having explained my quest, I was given the name and number of local historian Gareth Winter. I telephoned him that evening and told him I was researching the name Cave. He immediately said he knew a considerable amount about Augustus William Cave or 'AW' as he was known affectionately in local history circles. He suggested we meet in the Library in 10 minutes time and luckily Arthur Dew, my host at our farm stay in Pokohiwi Road, offered to drive us there.

What a surprise awaited us. We looked at the cards giving references to the name Cave appearing in the local paper, the *Wairarapa Daily Times,* during the later years of the 19th century and, instead of the usual two or three cards per person, we found a drawer full of them. We started to look up the references and, when we found the appropriate paper, page and column, we photographed the result.

Christopher Pope at Caves Road, Masterton. Courtesy Wairarapa Times-Age.

There were many references to Augustus Cave's racehorses which had won various races at local meetings. There were advertisements for workers to clear the bush at his farm, trespass and planning notices and articles about his importation of a famous draught Clydesdale stallion called 'The MacGregor' from Southland. If this was not enough, there were also several books in which the name 'A W Cave' featured very prominently. We returned to our lodgings very late, very tired, but very exhilarated.

The next day we went to Wellington, over a mountain range 60 miles to the south, in the hope of finding the wills of either Augustus William Cave or his wife Mary Ann Cave. We were unsuccessful but, amazingly, David Bilbrough who we spoke to at the National Archives told us he lived in a farming district near Masterton called Gladstone, and he thought he had some photos of Augustus and his horse which he would bring to us next Saturday. This he did and we were thrilled when he said we could keep them.

The third day we spent at Masterton Library looking more thoroughly at the books which mentioned A W Cave. We also tried to pinpoint the exact location of his farm, 'Woodleigh', although the house had burned to the ground a long time ago. We were also very excited to find there was a Caves Road in the area where my ancestor had purchased 243 acres of land in 1869 and 1972. That evening the Dews took us to Caves Road but we were still unable to pinpoint the exact location of the old farmhouse. It was, however, interesting to note that the National Sheepdog Trials had been held for several years on this land, formerly owned by my relatives.

The fourth day was a Saturday and first of all Kathy and I decided to revisit the local tourist office to thank them for all their help. There were several ladies working at their desks and we approached the one we judged to be in charge. She listened intently to our story and successful researches and then came out with the bombshell that she had gone to school with a Margaret Cave, who had married

Margaret Cave, with Christopher Pope wearing the historic waistcoat.

a Mr Thomas. She telephoned Margaret Thomas and made an appointment for us to see her early that afternoon. This was a wonderful piece of luck, made even more remarkable by the fact that she only worked part-time on one Saturday every four weeks at the tourist office and had also been away ill for several months. We had just happened to pick the one day that she was working.

One of the reference books Gareth Winter showed us at the library on our first night in Masterton was *A Meeting of Gentlemen on Matters Agricultural:*

the Masterton Show 1871-1986. The author Angus McCallum lived locally so, as we now had a few hours to spare, I telephoned him and inquired if he still had any copies of his book. He replied there were only a few copies left but would be very pleased to sell me one and suggested we come up to his house to collect it. My great-grand-uncle, Augustus William Cave, was president of the Agricultural and Pastoral Association at Masterton on two separate occasions, and had also been the patron for several years. The book contained several photographs of him, including one in 1890 when he was a member of the committee of the society. The committee members all had beards or long moustaches and were wearing various hats; a dog sat in front, and the whole scene was so very informal – they certainly looked the part of real pioneers. The book also had many references about Augustus which I found most interesting and stimulating and I shall treasure it the rest of my life.

Our call to Margaret Thomas' house turned out to be a truly emotional visit. I immediately discovered we were related through William Cave. He was my maternal great-great-grandfather and he was her paternal great-grandfather. William Cave, who married Caroline Mills on May 24 1838, had in addition to Augustus William Cave, who was born in 1840, a daughter Mary Elizabeth born in 1842, who was my great-grandmother, and another son, John Chamberlain Cave, born in 1855. John C Cave was Margaret's grandfather. She produced many photographs and newspaper cuttings and I spent several interesting hours poring over them. She had many fascinating stories to tell me about the Caves in New Zealand and I was able to give her some more details about her ancestors in England. She also gave me the telephone number of Kathleen Cave in England and when I phoned her later we were able to swap information on the Caves' family tree.

Then we had another enormous surprise. We knew from a newspaper cutting in the library that at the funeral of William Cave in 1896, a well known local Maori woman, Katerina Wi Waka, had placed a large Maori rug over his coffin as it was lowered into the grave, as a mark of deep sympathy and great respect. This was a particularly exciting discovery given the importance of Maori culture in a country where about 10 percent of the population are of Maori descent. Margaret now told us that Barbara Nichols, née Iorns, a descendent of Joseph Masters, the founder of Masterton, was coming shortly with a wonderful surprise. This turned out to be the waistcoat presented over 100 years ago by the Maori of Te Ore Ore to Augustus William Cave. The waistcoat was made from long, evenly stripped blades of flax, and gentian violet had been used to dye some of the strips, creating a very effective pattern. Aware of the Maori belief that the spirit of the person to whom the garment was given lives on in it, I must admit I experienced a very strange sensation when I was invited to try the waistcoat on.

Shortly afterwards, the waistcoat went on loan to the Museum of New Zealand, Te Papa Tongarewa, in Wellington, for five years and in December 2003 it was given to Aratoi in Masterton by Barbara Nichols. So it is now in the permanent collection of Wairarapa's museum of art and history.

A & P Association committee in early 1890s. Augustus Cave, president, centre of front row.

The next day we invited Margaret out for Sunday lunch and on the way to the restaurant she suggested we visit the Caves' town house. It was a very large, attractive colonial type villa and it was here they retired when they gave up farming. The new owners were restoring the building to its former glory since, sadly, some time ago it was converted into four flats. They were very interested to hear of the history of the villa and Margaret was able to recount many stories about the property. She remembered visiting Mary Ann Cave on numerous occasions when she was a little girl. She showed us the hall where the old grandfather clock stood, and part of the coving cut to accommodate it was still visible. The new owners showed us the house's nameplate – 'Nympsfield' – and said they had often wondered why it was so named. They were delighted when I told them I was 99.9 percent sure the house was named after the village in the Cotswolds where the family home 'Field Farm' was situated.

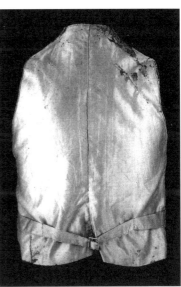

In the afternoon we visited the showgrounds of the Agricultural and Pastoral Association, the organisation Augustus had been president and patron of for several years. As soon as we entered the old pavilion we saw on the walls several large, framed photographs of Augustus and his various committees, including the excellent 1890 one. I remarked to the secretary that it would be wonderful if we could laser these photos so we could hang them up in our house in England, and I asked if there was any way we could do this. In England I would probably have had to write to the committee and sign various documents to remove these photographs but, to my complete surprise, the secretary said we could take them away to copy. English friends, who were staying in Masterton for several weeks, promised to return them when the copying had been done. This friendliness and helpfulness was typical of the way we have always been treated by New Zealanders.

The waistcoat presented to Augustus Cave by Te Ore Ore Maori. Front (above) and back (below).

On the final full day of our stay in Masterton we went to the town's Court House and were delighted to get copies of the wills of Augustus William and Mary Ann Cave. As they left no children these wills were long and very complicated and the estates included a whole host of beneficiaries. That evening we had a dinner party at the Dews with our friends from England, Alan and Nonnie Duncan, and archivist Gareth Winter, to celebrate our success. During a very pleasant evening Gareth asked if he could write an article about my Cave family researches. I agreed but had not expected a double page spread in the *Wairarapa Times Age*. The article was headed "An Englishman comes to Masterton to Discover his Roots" and subtitled "Climbing the Family Tree". It began: "Family research normally leads New Zealanders to search for their ancestors in England. Gareth Winter from the Wairarapa Archive reports on a recent reversal, where an Englishman came looking for his family."

Sadly, early next morning, we had to leave Masterton for the very long drive back to Auckland to catch the plane the following day to Australia. We both felt very exhilarated from the events of the last six days in Masterton. It seemed to us that someone had been watching over us and guiding us during those last few days. Masterton is now a special place in our hearts and we both knew, as we sped north along the main road, we were definitely going to return.

During the next three months we had a marvellous holiday seeing turtles laying their eggs on the beach at Heron Island on the Great Barrier Reef, whales diving in the deep at Kaikoura, penguins returning to the sea at dawn at Dunedin, albatrosses gliding in the sky – not to mention my paragliding adventure from the top of a mountain at Akaroa near Christchurch. But, in the end, none of these compared with the excitement and exhilaration of all the discoveries we made in Masterton.

Later, back home, I thought some people might be interested in my success in locating relatives in New Zealand, and encouraged to start delving into their own family trees. So with the help of Mrs Pat Hewertson, a local writer who submits weekly articles to the Plymouth newspaper *The Herald*, I wrote an article entitled "On a trip to the other side of the World, Chris strikes family gold".

CHAPTER 3

ANOTHER JOURNEY

Our next world trip in 2000 was to celebrate our 60th birthdays. I was very keen to return to New Zealand to continue my researches and, as the Olympic Games were being held in Sydney, it was an opportunity I could not resist. In addition, Kathy wanted to go to the Galapagos Islands for her birthday treat.

First, we visited China and went on an organised tour to Beijing, the Great Wall of China and the Warriors at Xian. Next, we did a house swap with a couple, Chitose and Masaru in Osaka, Japan, where we had a most enjoyable and unusual time. We slept on the floor on a thin mattress at their house and at the Mt Koya Temple, high up in the mountains. Eating off very low tables was not easy and not recommended for people with bad knees, a bad back, or for very tall people like myself at six feet five inches!

At the Olympics we watched 33 different events during the 16 days of competition. We were lucky enough to sit amongst the Queally family and share their absolute delight when their son, Jason Queally, won Britain's first gold medal of the Games for cycling. Kathy Freeman's night at the

Kathy and Christopher Pope on the Great Wall of China.

Olympic stadium was certainly an experience we will never forget; but seeing Steve Redgrave win his fifth gold medal in successive Olympics was undoubtedly the highlight. Another fascinating aspect of the Olympics was the different people you dined with while waiting for an event to start. We spoke with Russians, Poles, Swedes and people from many other nations but I particularly remember a chat with an Iraqi couple who had escaped from their country because of

Title deed for 1872
purchase of land from
Maori.

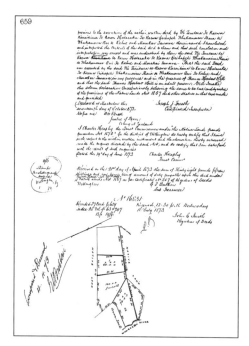

Saddam Hussein. The wife, with a yashmak over her face, could not speak a word of English, but her husband explained they were very sad to have left behind their parents and many brothers and sisters. They worried about their fate and he said some of them would by now have been taken prisoner, tortured and killed.

Next stop was New Zealand and after brief visits to Auckland and the Bay of Islands, where we were very fortunate to see the end of the Lindauer Coastal Classic Yacht Race, and Rotorua, we arrived – for the second time – in Masterton. This time I had booked accommodation about 15 kilometres outside the town. From the brochure it looked a very peaceful place where Kathy could possibly relax while I continued my researches. As soon as we turned into the drive, I realised I had made a splendid choice – it was a real gem of a place. A bungalow nestled in its own valley and looked out onto two beautiful lakes and the gardens were superb with wild ducks and birds feeding on the water. Now I felt I could venture off during the next few days to continue my researches knowing Kathy would be happy relaxing there.

The next morning I visited my relative Margaret Thomas for a lengthy conversation about her side of the Cave family tree. She then gave me a photograph of my great-great-grandfather William Cave and the loving cup he brought out from England, presumably as a present for his son. I was absolutely thrilled to have these for I had, up to that time, never seen a photograph of William Cave. Next I visited Gareth Winter to see if there was any chance I might find the deed relating to the transaction when, according to *The Cyclopedia of New Zealand* of 1897, Augustus William Cave bought 900 acres at Te Ore Ore in 1870. Gareth gave me a few hints about where to look in the Land Registry in Wellington but said the chances of finding any documentation were not very promising.

Next morning I rose at 5.20 am, caught the 6.42 train to Wellington and arrived at the Land Registry at 9 o'clock just as it was opening. It took me some time to follow the system of ledgers and maps but once I had mastered it, I really began to make progress. A couple of hours later I found the first deed, 'Rangitumau Block' Sections 65-66-67. Augustus William Cave purchased 270 acres on July 21 1878 for £675.00 from Mr McRae Drummond. Soon afterwards I found the sale documentation when he sold the same land on March 28 1907 for £2,556.00 to the Shaw brothers. This land is at the end of Caves Road. Although I was pretty sure Augustus had bought land surrounding 'Soldiers Settlement Road', as it was called on old maps, and possibly also bought land from the Maori, I needed documentation to support my theories.

Suddenly at 3.30 pm, half an hour before the Land Registry closed, I hit the jackpot. I found the deeds detailing Augustus buying 100 acres on December 17 1869

Wi Tinitara Te Kaewa.

for £250 and 143 acres on October 17 1872 for £357 from local Maori. The heading of the second deed says:
"Dated the seventeenth day of October 1872
Wi Tinitara and Others
Aboriginal Natives
To
Mr A W Cave
Conveyance 11144."
This land is described as 'Te Ahitanga Block' No 2 and it surrounded 'Soldiers Settlement Road'. The other Maori names, referred to in the heading, are detailed in the actual Conveyance.

I could not believe my luck and I was really pleased I had taken the trouble to be at the Land Registry early. If I had not done so, I would have missed finding these deeds documenting the sales by local Maori. Quickly I made arrangements for the second of these deeds to be lasered by a specialist company and a copy sent to me in England. I must admit, as I travelled back by train to Masterton that night, I felt very pleased with the progress I had made that day, as I had established a further connection with the local Maori, besides the gift of the waistcoat.

When I visited Gareth Winter the next morning, he congratulated me on my success at the Land Registry. We had a general chat about the progress of my researches and Gareth thought that, in those days, it had been unusual for a farmer's son to go to a grammar school. But, according to *The Cyclopedia of New Zealand*, Augustus attended Dursley Grammar School. I told Gareth I would like to know the exact location of Augustus' farmhouse called 'Woodleigh' which had been completely destroyed by fire some time after 1904. 'Woodleigh' was marked on some maps, but I said I would like proof of its exact location. Gareth said this might be difficult, but I should start by driving down Soldiers Settlement Road to see if I could find any evidence. There I met James McKay, who told me his ancestors had first travelled to Dunedin and then to Masterton, arriving at approximately the same time as Augustus. He said he was fairly sure 'Woodleigh' had been situated where I had imagined it to be and suggested I contact Neil Stuart.

I phoned Neil Stuart who immediately invited Kathy and me to his house that afternoon, and what a surprise awaited us. It turned out his wife Beryl and I were distantly related by marriage. Joseph Masters, the founder of Masterton, had two daughters, the elder of whom was christened Sarah Bourton. Her first marriage was to Richard Iorns and they had a daughter called Mary Ann who married Augustus. Sarah's second marriage was to Henry Bannister and they had several sons, one of whom was Edwin who, in turn, had a daughter Mildred, who was Beryl's mother. It was even more amazing that Beryl's husband Neil had been gradually purchasing the land surrounding Soldiers Settlement Road including all the land originally owned by Augustus and, of course, the site of 'Woodleigh'. In the old days small 40 acre plots of land were economic, but in modern times farms had needed much larger acreages.

Beryl also produced photos and newspaper cuttings, some of which she very kindly gave to me. After a cup of tea we were taken to see her son, who showed us a lovely drawing of Augustus done on November 20 1911 by Miss Edna Bannister when she was 16. It was an excellent likeness with Augustus looking very much like the photographs we had seen of him. I also discovered that afternoon when I studied Beryl's family tree how many of her ancestors had Masters as a forename. Beryl had been born Beryl Masters Henderson and her mother Mildred Sarah Masters Bannister – and one of her relatives had the forename of Woodleigh. Her ancestors were obviously very proud of the Masters connection and rightly so.

There were more surprises early the next morning. I was woken about 5 am with the windows rattling and first thought there was a thunderstorm. But when I felt a violent shaking I realised what was happening. We were in the midst of an earthquake and we heard on the radio a few hours later that it was strength five, quite a substantial shake. According to our host Glenys Hansen, the area experiences about three of these earthquakes per year. When I came for breakfast Glenys was busy checking her ornaments for breakages; luckily she had not sustained much damage. New Zealand is on a fault line and I am told there is about one chance in five Wellington will suffer a major earthquake within the next 50 years. In fact, government buildings in Wellington have been specially designed and built to withstand such an event. I also learnt some time later that during the very bad earthquake of 1942, the Cave's town house in Short Street, Masterton, suffered a great deal and the house came off its foundation pillars.

Augustus had always been very keen on racehorses and had a private training track at 'Woodleigh'. He bred, owned and raced many racehorses and *The Cyclopedia of New Zealand* states: "In local meetings Mr Cave's colours have often forged their way to the front, the wins being always most popular". As he held the office of president and then later in life became the patron of the Masterton Racing Club, I decided to visit the track to see if I could find any records or mention of his name. The groundsman was most helpful and for about two hours we searched the storeroom where all the records were kept. We found records going back to 1921 but nothing relating to the 1890s when Augustus' horses ran. The racecourse is now used only for training because a drop in attendances has meant insufficient income to finance the upkeep required to comply with the very tight fire rules and regulations introduced in New Zealand. The old pavilion, the finishing post and winners board and the stewards' boxes are still in their original positions, but look a little jaded. Still, it was nice to sit up in the old pavilion in the seats marked 'Committee Members Only' and imagine what Augustus must have seen when a race meeting was in full swing.

On our last morning I decided to return to the library and search again through the cards and the *Wairarapa Daily Times* to see if I could find any more items relating to Augustus. It was fortunate I did, for I discovered another obituary notice which filled me with much pride as I read it. It was a short, well written notice. If my obituary, I thought, contained just a few of the attributes mentioned in his, I would have achieved much in life. It read:

> "As a farmer he was industrious and painstaking; as a
> neighbour he was incomparable; as a sportsman he
> was honest and straightforward and always played
> the game and as a friend he was the embodiment
> of fidelity."

With this glowing obituary, the Maori waistcoat and land purchase and Augustus' stature in the development of Masterton, I felt his life was one that should be written about. I consulted Gareth Winter, the archivist, about this and he readily agreed to help me in any way he could. It is said there is one book in everybody and I felt the life of Augustus William Cave and the early years of Masterton was my book and my story to tell.

As Kathy and I continued our wonderful holiday round the world, I started to make notes and formulate ideas for the book. We flew from Auckland to Buenos Aires, and after a short break in this fabulous city, we continued on to Igassu Falls, which were even more spectacular than the Victoria Falls, and then on to Rio de Janeiro. After this we flew to La Paz and journeyed overland to Cuzco and the Inca lost city of Machu Picchu. Finally we travelled to the Galapagos Islands, the highlight of the holiday for Kathy.

CHAPTER 4

ON THE FAMILY TRAIL

After I had been home a few months I realised I would need much more information to write a satisfactory life story of A W Cave, so I started planning yet another world tour – our third. To give Kathy something special to enjoy while we were away, I had always tried to plan my 'family research holidays' to coincide with a big sporting event such as the Olympic Games in Sydney. Fortuitously, the America's Cup was to be sailed on Auckland harbour in February 2003, so I started to plan our trip around this event.

On our way to New Zealand in January 2003 we spent a fabulous week in the Cook Islands. One day we travelled by small boat to a beautiful island with lovely palm trees surrounded by white sand and green clear water which had been used in the TV series 'Shipwreck'. On the way back our guide said one of the first Englishmen to come to the Cook Islands was Joseph Marsters from Derbyshire and there were many descendants of his living in the islands. I nearly fell off my seat for Joseph Masters was the founder of Masterton. He was born in Derby in 1802 and although the name is spelt slightly differently, it would not surprise me if these two men were related. In the old days, when many spelt poorly, if they could read or write at all, names had a habit of changing slightly.

In New Zealand we did a repeat house and car swap with Trevor and Joy Riley from Albany, 15 miles north of Auckland. The first week we travelled to the Bay of Islands and the very north of New Zealand and the second week to Masterton via the Coromandel Peninsula and Napier. At our Napier bed and breakfast our hostess mentioned that she was judging the Pony and Trap Competition at a big show next week – and when I asked where, she said it was at Masterton. This was another of those coincidences which seemed to occur quite frequently in New Zealand for it was the Masterton Show we were coming especially to see, because Augustus had been for many years the Patron and President of the A & P (Agricultural and Pastoral) Society which organises the show.

For the first five days of our Masterton stay we were the guests of my new-found relative, Beryl Stuart and her husband Neil whom we had met on our second visit to the Wairarapa. They were wonderful hosts and took us to many places.

The first morning we went to what they believed was the site of Augustus' old farmhouse 'Woodleigh'. When I saw the position and the splendid, very large old oak tree standing proudly nearby, I was almost 100 percent certain that this, indeed, was the site of his home. Augustus had never forgotten his English roots. As Charles Bannister wrote in his book *Early History of the Wairarapa*: "Sparrows were first brought to Masterton by Mr A W Cave in the middle sixties. They reminded him of his home in England so he decided to give some a free ride to Masterton." So I think it reasonable to assume that in the bush near his home he would have planted this oak tree to remind him of his farmhouse in the English Cotswolds.

Beryl gave me some newspaper cuttings for my scrapbook and also a photograph of the first Post Office in Masterton. With the horses hitched up outside, the rough

Augustus Cave, seated right of doorway, with family at 'Woodleigh' in 1904.

road and the dress of the townsfolk, it looked like a set for a Wild West movie, but to me it had greater significance. This was the actual general store built by Joseph Masters and Richard Iorns where Sarah Bourton, Augustus' mother-in-law, became the first postmistress.

In the afternoon I went to see Margaret Thomas and took some photocopies of documents and pictures acquired since I last saw her. She, in turn, produced a wonderful photo album her sister had lent her. It was inscribed with the words: "A happy and enjoyable visit to Woodleigh – M Douglas, January to March 1904. Now,

Above: Augustus Cave with shire horses. Below: Pony and trap, with windmill in background. Both photographs from 1904.

for the first time, I was able to look at 'Woodleigh' farmhouse and it was indeed a lovely building with a veranda going round two sides of the house. There was Augustus, aged 64, sitting on a chair surrounded by his friends with their young children. Mr Douglas was very industrious and painstaking in his taking of photographs. Besides some of Augustus' racehorses, there were shots of his shire horses and one of a pony and trap by his windmill. There were also pictures of his other animals including his sheep and one with Augustus and his wife feeding hens. There were some very fine family photographs and an interesting one of a Maori family group. As well, he had taken pictures showing a working farm. There was a splendid photo of Augustus with his dog by the threshing machine and in another he and a child are with some men loading hay with pitchforks. Finally there was a superb photograph of a large social gathering: a group of ladies sitting by the water in which some children are playing, with other people on a bridge overlooking the scene.

I spent much of the second day at the library going through the microfilm of the *Wairarapa Daily Times* from 1865 to 1890, in case there was something in the paper not recorded on the reference cards. After about three hours, I discovered a long article that had not been recorded and it certainly proved the accuracy of Augustus' obituary. Victorians had a habit of embellishing things such as obituaries so it was possible that what was said in his obituary was not true. But after reading this article, a record of speeches made by settlers and town dignitaries who knew Augustus very well, I was reassured his obituary was indeed true. Some 50 settlers and residents of Masterton had assembled to bid farewell and give him a present prior to his departure for a trip to England. This trip was the first time he had returned to the 'Old Country' since he had emigrated about 40 years earlier. A number of people spoke including the Mayor who said, "The town owed a great deal to Mr Cave" and "Mr Cave's name as President of the Racing Club was a sufficient guarantee of the integrity of this Club". Another settler, Edwin Meredith, stated, "He was one of the best and strongest allies in starting the A & P Association. He was also a conspicuous member of the Racing Club as a man who always ran straight." These were fine words and it was now obvious to me that Augustus had definitely been a well respected and much loved member of the local community.

Piri Te Tau, Christopher Pope, Jim Rimene and Gareth Winter on Te Ore Ore marae.

On the third morning, Gareth Winter and I went to the local Maori iwi's office. We were greeted most warmly and an appointment was made for Gareth, my wife and me to go to the local tribal meeting place, or 'marae', at Te Ore Ore early the next morning. I was thrilled and looked forward to this meeting with much excitement. In the afternoon Beryl and Neil drove us to Martinborough, the wine growing centre of the Wairarapa. It was a very pleasant and interesting trip. In the evening we went to an open air concert in the local park. The standard of the music and singing was first-class and we thoroughly enjoyed ourselves.

I woke early the next morning anticipating the prospect of finding out more about Augustus' connection with the local Maori. We met Gareth at 9 o'clock and then proceeded to the Te Ore Ore marae where Piri Te Tau and Jim Rimene greeted us. Piri Te Tau was, I gather, in charge of the marae and related to Katerina Wi Waka, the local dignitary who placed a Maori blanket over the coffin of William Cave, Augustus' father and my great-great-grandfather. Jim Rimene's ancestor Wi Tinitara Te Kaewa was the Maori chief who sold land to Augustus in 1872.

We sat on chairs on the marae and, after introductions, Jim Rimene told us his grandfather had worked for Augustus and had been the only person who could ride one of his stallions. He said that as Augustus' farm was very near the marae he would have provided food when they had a large gathering. I was so pleased to hear of this close connection between the two families. Piri Te Tau then gave me a photograph of Wi Tinitara Te Kaewa and said I could take it away to copy. I was extremely grateful for this as it tied in nicely with the copy of the conveyance certificate I had from the Maori chief's sale of some land to Augustus.

We were then taken inside and shown around the meeting house. On the walls were photographs of deceased dignitaries and I noted the one lent to us was the first on the wall just inside the door. We were told stories about some of the dignitaries, particularly about one who attended the Coronation of King Edward VII as a standard bearer for one of the dukes. There was also a feathered cloak hanging over the door to the kitchen. I mentioned the waistcoat given by the Maori of the marae to Augustus and said I was extremely proud of it. Piri Te Tau thought the waistcoat was very rare and he inquired if I could return it to them; sadly I had to tell him the matter was out of my hands. I explained that Augustus had only one child who died at the age of six and because Augustus died before his wife, all his estate, including the waistcoat, had passed to his widow and thereafter to her heirs. Barbara Nichols, née Iorns, now owned Augustus' waistcoast.

Piri Te Tau then asked if Kathy and I would like to return in two days' time, when children from the local school were to be welcomed formally onto the marae. We immediately agreed and thanked him. We left soon afterwards and Gareth suggested that on Thursday we might like to meet at the school itself and then come officially with the children to the marae.

I spent the rest of the day at the library and at the bookshop, working out which books of reference I would need to write my early history of Masterton. In the end I decided to purchase *Early History of the Wairarapa* by Charles Bannister, which had many references to Augustus Cave, and *North of the Waingawa* by Ian F Grant, which was full of dates and interesting information. One important book

Harvest time at 'Woodleigh'.

with a lot of detail about the early years was *Masterton's First Hundred Years* by A G Bagnall, but unfortunately it was out of print. As there was bound to be some information I would need for my project in the book, I went to the library and took photocopies of a number of pages. This took some time but I thought I had better not leave any stone unturned because New Zealand is a long way from England and, if I needed clarification on some event, I couldn't just pop down to the library to get the information!

Late in the afternoon I called into the Wairarapa Archive and Gareth told me the teacher in charge of the marae visit would be very happy if we went with them in the official party. In turn, I told him I was very pleased that I had found a photograph in one of the books of a bridge named the Caves Bridge Crossing. Augustus had had a serious accident on Abbotts Bridge, just outside Featherston, when he worked in the early days as a driver of a wagon train bringing in provisions to the town, and I assumed that was why this crossing was named after him. Gareth asked where the bridge was and I said the caption on the photograph stated, "Featherston side of the Rimutaka Range from the Caves Bridge crossing". Immediately he said there was another person called Cave living near Featherston and the bridge could have been named after him. Sometimes, when you have an archivist who is so knowledgeable and who so enjoys his work, his great accumulation of facts can work against you! Of course, on so many other occasions I have been so grateful for his help, and his information has been of great assistance to me.

We left the 'House of Stuart' the following morning and moved for a few days to the superb B & B where we had stayed on our previous visit. Our host, Glenys Hansen, told us that a family of black swans had now come to her lake and was living there very peacefully. After a quick lunch we set off for Hiona School where we were met by Gareth. He introduced us to Peta Campbell, who was in charge of the group going to the marae. She asked us if we would like to see the children practising the greeting songs they were going to sing there and we readily agreed. We were ushered into the assembly hall where the teacher, who taught Maori culture at the school, was giving the children a lecture with particular reference to the songs they were going to sing and the significance of the greeting at the entrance to the marae. They then sang the two songs, both in Maori, with a great deal of gusto. Kathy and I were very impressed. After singing the songs again we all set off to the marae and arrived some 20 minutes later.

Benches were set out on the marae and we were ushered to the front and seated by Peta Campbell's husband, Mick Ludden. Opposite us, sitting on the verandah of the meeting house, were three Maori. The ceremony started with the children singing their two songs and then Mick Ludden spoke in Maori for about seven minutes. The senior Maori then replied and during the speech Mick nudged me and whispered that he was talking about me and my great-grand-uncle Augustus. This speech also lasted quite a time. Next, the headmaster said a few words in English and then slowly placed an envelope on the ground which the head Maori picked up. Then we were all assembled, with ourselves near the front, to exchange the traditional Maori greeting of touching noses (known as 'hongi') with each of the three Maori present and finally we entered the meeting house.

Inside, we sat on a bench near the door and all the children squatted on the floor. One of the Maori then gave a talk in English about the meeting house which was most interesting, and in reply Peta Campbell thanked him for his hospitality. Finally she gave a long list of the marae's rules and regulations and what the children might and might not do. The formalities over, the children went out to play and we went with Peta and her husband into the kitchen to watch the children's meal being prepared and to have a chat over a cup of tea. Some time later, more staff arrived from the school to help with the meal and when Mick Ludden departed, we decided to go with him since Kathy was feeling very tired.

On the journey home to our B & B, we reflected on a super day and how lucky and privileged we had been to experience a real marae visit and not a tourist version. Also, it was amazing to think it was this Te Ore Ore marae that Augustus had visited, probably many times, wearing, as Gareth remarked, the special waistcoat the local Maori had made for him. As I told Gareth the next day, the visit to the marae, and the meeting with Jim Rimene and Piri Te Tau, were certainly the highlights of our holiday and experiences we would always treasure.

(A few months later, I received a copy of an excellent article written by Owen Winter and published in the *Wairarapa Times-Age* on May 21 2003 about our meeting with Jim and Piri and the visit to the marae with the local school and I thought the heading "Marae visit a highlight for a family researcher" to be most apt.)

The next day there was another occasion I had been particularly looking forward to: the A & P Association Show, which Augustus had been so involved in. My two previous visits had not coincided with this event, so this was our first opportunity to visit Masterton's A & P Show.

Before I went to the Showgrounds I had arranged to see Barbara Nichols at the Wairarapa branch of the New Zealand Genealogical Society. She was most helpful and gave me photographs and newspaper cuttings about Augustus' wife Mary Ann, articles about her mother Sarah Bourton and information about the Iorns family in general. Also she gave me a newspaper article about Mary Anne's father entitled, "How Richard Iorns dug his own grave".

The main feature of the Show was to be the entry of 1,000 Harley Davidson motorbikes due to arrive at 11.45 am. I left Barbara at about 11.30 am, met Kathy who had been shopping, and we took up our position on the main road just outside the Showgrounds. About 10 minutes later we heard in the distance the roar of engines, which became louder and louder as they approached until suddenly we saw four police cars followed by the bikers about 10 abreast across the road. It was a wonderful sight as they passed by quite slowly, spectators cheering and bikers waving back. The bikes carried flags of many nations. Amazingly, they just kept on coming and it took 15 minutes for them all to pass.

The Show itself was very entertaining and I particularly remember the international wood chopping match between American and New Zealand women. I sat in the old pavilion and tried to imagine the scene Augustus would have looked out on all those years ago. Competitions like the horse-jumping and riding were probably similar, but the fashions would have been entirely different. I have a superb photograph of the Showgrounds in 1910 with lady spectators in long dresses and the men in bowler hats, so very different from today's dress of jeans and t-shirts.

In the evening our friends from England, Alan and Nonnie Duncan, joined us for dinner at the B & B, and the next morning we set off on the long drive back to Auckland. The following day a Fullers boat took us out on the water to see a race in the America's Cup. It was an interesting day but tinged with sadness as the Swiss boat *Alinghi*, skippered by the very experienced New Zealander Russell Coutts, beat the New Zealand entry. Two days later we went out with Fullers again but the race was cancelled. We were told there was not enough wind at the end of the course and the light breeze was not blowing in the right direction. This all seemed very strange as the wind was blowing quite hard where we stood on the deck and it would have been the same conditions for both boats.

From New Zealand we flew first to Perth where we had a most pleasant stay with our New Zealand friend Simon Dorset, who had booked us an apartment right on the waterfront at Scarborough.

Then we took a flight to India for a short but fascinating visit. I was able to film a Hindu wedding which lasted from 1.00- 5.00 am, and ride on an elephant.

We arrived back at Heathrow a week later feeling very satisfied with a wonderful holiday, and for obtaining sufficient information to have enough material to write a book about the life of Augustus William Cave. I was determined to write this book in the hope that others would be encouraged to start tracing their own family trees. I cannot guarantee the outcome will be as satisfactory as my own experiences, but you will never know until you try. But I can guarantee that you will meet fascinating people and discover interesting facts on the road to researching a family tree. Little did I realise when I started some 13 years ago that I would end up in the very beautiful country of New Zealand and have this very special Maori connection. I feel I have been lucky enough to strike gold and, who knows, a similar result may await other family researchers.

CHAPTER 5

EARLY HISTORY OF MASTERTON FROM 1841 TO 1861

The first European to explore the Wairarapa was the surveyor Robert Stokes in 1841. He reported that the Maori were very friendly, the area was well watered and would be excellent for grazing stock. The beginnings of Masterton township took place in May 1854, the result of negotiations between the Maori chief Retimana Te Korou and an Englishman called Joseph Masters.

Joseph Masters was born in Derby, England in 1802. He had a colourful and varied career in his early years. After serving an apprenticeship as a cooper, he became a gaoler, a policeman and finally a soldier in the Grenadier Guards. He married Sarah Bourton in 1826 and six years later he emigrated with his wife and first daughter to Tasmania, where he found employment as a cooper in the whaling industry. He then returned to being a gaoler while farming a small plot of land.

Joseph Masters.

In 1841 Masters came with his family to New Zealand and settled in Wellington where he worked as a cooper and as a general store keeper on Lambton Quay. His wife and their younger daughter also engaged in business as straw bonnet manufacturers.

Masters was concerned the working people of Wellington did not have easy access to farmland and he was upset when he learned the government, after purchasing large areas of the Wairarapa from the Maori, might then sell the land to large landowners.

Joseph Masters believed that men with only small amounts of capital should be allowed to buy land in New Zealand. One way to do this was for groups of working men to pool together and buy a large block of land which they could then subdivide amongst their membership. Each member would take a one acre section in a central urban area and a 40 acre farm on the outskirts of the town.

So in December 1852 Masters began a campaign to raise awareness about the issue, writing a series of letters to the *Wellington Independent* and to the other local newspapers, promoting his idea of small farm settlements. He called a meeting in March 1853 at the Crown and Anchor Hotel on the beach at Lambton Quay, and the Small Farms' Association consisting mainly of Hutt and Wellington settlers, was formed. He suggested establishing a town in the fertile flat lands of the Wairarapa plain. His ideas were readily accepted by the working people of Wellington, many of whom had been enticed to emigrate to New Zealand with the promise of cheap land, a dream that had not materialised.

A short time later Joseph Masters and Charles Carter, who held similar views, had an interview with Sir George Grey, the governor who was about to introduce new land regulations on the instructions of Earl Grey, the colonial minister in London. Governor Grey listened to their ideas for a scheme for settlement in the Wairarapa and said he was happy to support the scheme as long as the local Maori were prepared to sell the land in question.

Joseph Masters and Henry Jackson, another member of the Small Farms' Association and a blunt, Maori-speaking farmer, went together across the Rimutaka Ranges that separate Wellington from the Wairarapa to select suitable land for their projected settlement. Their journey was arduous and it took five days to reach the banks of the Waingawa River. At the village of Ngamutawa they went to see the chief of Rangitane, Retimana Te Korou, who had been born towards the end of the 18th century, and his son-in-law Ihaiah Whakamairu. The chief and his son-in-law listened very carefully to what the settlers had to say and agreed to consider the matter. The chief consulted with his family and other local chiefs and agreed with the scheme in principle, mainly because the Maori could see the benefit of the settlers opening shops on land near their villages. Also the Wairarapa Maori were not numerous and they had only just returned to their ancestral lands after being forced to flee for eight years by Te Ati Awa and other Wellington area iwi. It was on this trip that Masters and Jackson chose the site for Masterton, Masters describing it as "the gem spot of the valley". On their return to Wellington with Ihaiah, the necessary deeds were signed and the government purchased the land in December 1853 and January 1854.

Sir George Grey had been concerned about the spread of leasehold agreements in the Wairarapa and had intervened personally. In August 1853 he met with Maori and the leaseholders and, after much discussion and argument, he managed to persuade both parties that the sale of land was the best solution. By the end of September, the Commissioner of Crown Lands had negotiated sales of about 500,000 acres, nearly all in the South Wairarapa, for approximately £4,000. Some of the sale proceeds were set aside for Maori schools and a hospital and for annuities for the chiefs who sold the land.

Masters and the Small Farms' Association had chosen two sites for their scheme. One was named Greytown after Sir George and the other Masterton, named by the settlers for Joseph Masters. When the settlements were laid out, the Small Farms' Association purchased the whole town block of Masterton from the government at 10 shillings an acre and balloted 200 one acre sections to their members for £1 each. The difference in price was for surveying and other costs. These town acres were on both sides of the main road which later became Queen Street, and were in the form of a cross with a vertical arm going from the Waipoua River to the Kuripuni Stream. After selecting a town acre, members of the Association had the right to select a rural section of 40 acres at 10 shillings an acre. A ballot for sections in Masterton was held in mid-March 1854 and 30 potential settlers immediately applied for sections. The ballot for Masterton's 40 acre sites was held on April 19 and 63 out of the 100 lots were applied for.

On May 6 1854 the first party of settlers set out from Wellington to take up their balloted lands in Masterton. The party consisted of David Dixon, Michael Dixon (no relation) and his daughter Emma, and John Cole together with 37 cattle and all their worldly possessions stowed on bullocks. Their progress was very slow, particularly on the very hazardous track over the Rimutakas. After crossing the Moroa Plain they were forced to rest for five days as the Ruamahanga River was in full flood. Eventually they were able to swim their cattle across the river and they followed in canoes. They then travelled north and eventually reached the site destined to become Masterton on May 21. They were greeted by Ihaiah Whakamairu who provided them with food and gave them shelter for the night.

The first settlers spent the next few days exploring the area and the land earmarked for the new town. They quickly discovered why the Maori called the area Whakaoriori (the evening birdsong, recalling a lullaby) – much of the land was covered with forest so dense there was no track through it. Charles and Mary Dixon, Henry Jones with his eldest son John, and Edward and Emily Eaton arrived soon afterwards and the early settlers set about the task of felling and sawing timber for their new houses.

To bring goods to Masterton, Joseph Masters frequently travelled back and forth across the Rimutakas with two pack bullocks. The journey from Masterton to Wellington took four days and consisted of travelling through mud, over mountains and wading and swimming rivers. He also regularly promoted Masterton's progress in the Wellington press. Problems arose when the Maori chiefs demanded payment for the trees needed for housing, but this problem was eventually solved.

Joseph Masters and Sarah Bourton had two daughters, Sarah born in 1827 and Mary in 1833. On April 22 1847 young Sarah married Richard Iorns who had arrived in Wellington in 1842 and was subsequently in partnership with Joseph Masters as ginger beer manufacturers at Te Aro Flats. In 1854 the two men went to Masterton to build a house for the Iorns family. The house consisted of split slabs with a shingled roof, a clay chimney and calico windows.

The building of the house progressed well and by the beginning of 1855 it was ready for occupation by Iorns' wife and children. Richard gave a letter for his wife to Mr Dixon, travelling to Wellington for stores, saying he would soon be coming to collect her and the family. As Sarah was reading the letter, with her eldest child Mary Ann, there was a sudden tremor and rumbling beneath the house. They both dashed outside as the chimney crashed through the roof onto the chairs they had just been sitting on. Luckily the other three children were asleep in a room well away from the chimney and they were all lifted to safety through a window.

Wellington was devastated by the earthquake which had been severe enough to lift the seafront nine feet into the air. Sarah packed up what remained of her belongings and waited for her husband. He, in turn, came as fast as he could. On the way he examined the newly-cut track over the Rimutakas to see if it was still passable with pack animals, and decided it was. When Richard Iorns arrived in Wellington and saw the terrible damage done by the earthquake, he decided they must all return to Masterton immediately.

They packed two bullock loads of necessities and the rest of their possessions were left stored in the two undamaged rooms. Sarah had previously broken in a heifer to carry a pack and so they set off the next morning on the dangerous journey to Masterton, with the family riding on the cart and leading the two-year-old heifer. The journey started along the flat Hutt Road and everything went according to plan until the Hutt River had to be crossed by punt. The cart and luggage were put on the punt but the bullock refused to get on board so it and the heifer were forced to swim across. Safely across, the first night was spent at the Hutt.

Next day the party reached Mangaroa where there was accommodation. A couple of pack bullocks were waiting for them there and they were loaded the next morning. The most docile animal was chosen to carry the two boys, William Iorns aged five on one side and Joseph Iorns, three, on the other side of the animal. They were put in baskets filled with pillows to make them comfortable with Joseph's weighted as he was much lighter than his brother. When everything was loaded they set off with Sarah carrying the baby on her back in a shawl, taking the lead with the heifer. Next in line came Richard leading the bullock with the two boys. Then the second bullock, tied to the first animal with a long rope, and finally Mary Ann, aged seven, who walked all the way. They soon started to climb and the rough narrow track was very precipitous in places. It was very arduous climbing over the Rimutaka ranges and they stopped many times. At last they reached the top, and then they made their way down to Burling's accommodation house, where Featherston is now situated. The accommodation was very rough but very acceptable after such a hard journey over the mountains.

The following day they set out for Greytown and had a much easier time, the route being level, and that night they stayed at the home of Thomas Kempton, an early settler. They set off early next morning and travelled to Papawai, then crossed the seven branches of the Waiohine River. Unfortunately they experienced some very bad places and were bogged down in the swamps. Eventually they came out at nightfall where Parkvale is now situated and were met by Joseph Masters with his home-made bullock cart.

After crossing the Taratahi Plains they eventually reached Masterton at midnight, utterly exhausted but delighted to find a billy boiling and a supper laid out by Edward Eaton who lived not far away.

Reverend William Ronaldson.

When the Iorns family arose the next day, they were overjoyed to see such beautiful views outside. Soon afterwards Maori started to appear with gifts of potatoes, pork, pigeons and many other things to eat. They came in small numbers until the whole of the Ngaumutawa tribe had arrived. At this point they danced a haka of welcome and presented the gifts. The Maori then constructed an 'umu', or oven, and started cooking dinner. Next to arrive was the Reverend William Ronaldson, an Anglican minister and Maori missionary. He blessed the food in Maori and stayed for the feast. He interpreted all the speeches made by the Maori for the benefit of the Iorns family. After an amazing and unusual day for the family, the Maori left for their homes in the evening.

At this time there were only a few settlers in the area, all of them struggling to build a home and to clear enough land to cultivate wheat, potatoes and other crops. There was a great community spirit, with everyone helping each other and much assistance given to new arrivals. The settlers depended on the Maori to provide them with seeds with which to grow their crops. Richard Iorns immediately started work enlarging the house as he intended opening a shop on the premises, and later that year Masterton's first general store opened.

A short time later a report reached Masterton that a man had been drowned in the river and his feet were sticking out of the shingle. A party was organised to collect the body and Richard Iorns volunteered to dig the grave in land alongside the river, later the official cemetery. When the party arrived at the river they found no body, just a pair of old discarded boots sticking out of the mud. So the first grave in the cemetery was left empty, but sadly not for long. Shortly afterwards, on November 14 1855, Richard Iorns died and was buried in the grave he himself had dug. He was only 40 years old and, according to most reference books, he died of pneumonia, although the death certificate gave the cause of death as "disease of the heart".

Sarah Iorns was left with four young children and a store to run, and to her great credit she decided to stay on. The Maori came to her aid, helping her grow her own wheat, which was ground into flour with a small hand mill. She was then able to make bread, baking it in a camp oven. They also taught her to make arrowroot which was a good food for the children. This was done by gathering puha and grating large potatoes into a container, draining off the liquid and drying the residue in the sun. The arrowroot could also be mixed with eggs and milk and then browned in the oven to make a pudding.

Early in 1856 Sarah went to Wellington to attend to her late husband's affairs. She bought a horse and made the rough and hazardous journey on her own. Post Office officials there knew she and her husband had opened the

Richard Iorns' death certificate; the cause of death – "disease of the heart".

first general store in Masterton and they asked her if she was willing to undertake the duties of post mistress at a salary of £5 per year. She readily agreed and took back to Masterton the first mailbag containing just one letter. Her store became the first post office in Masterton.

In Wellington she bought some goods and arranged for them to be sent by cart to the top of the Rimutakas, where they were then transferred to Burlings. Her father collected them and brought the goods to Masterton on his bullock cart. On this journey to Wellington, a chance meeting was to greatly affect Sarah Iorns' life. When she passed a gang of men working on the Rimutaka road, she caught the interest of one of the workers, Henry Bannister. On her return trip to Masterton he gave her some lunch and asked if he could visit her on his next break and she agreed. When the time came, Henry Bannister did not return with his workmates to Wellington but travelled to Masterton. He called at Sarah Iorns' house and was invited in for a meal.

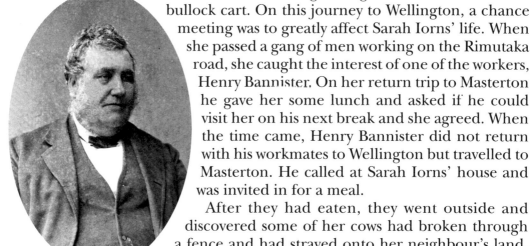

Henry Bannister.

After they had eaten, they went outside and discovered some of her cows had broken through a fence and had strayed onto her neighbour's land. Henry went to fetch the animals and was met by a very angry neighbour. Henry said that once the animals were rounded up and returned home, he would mend the fence. This assurance did not help the situation for the bachelor neighbour could plainly see that, at a time eligible females were a rarity in Masterton, he now had a rival for Sarah's affections.

They started to argue, the neighbour lost his temper and let fly with a fist. Henry retaliated and a full-blooded fight took place. Henry possessed some boxing skills and a blow to the nose, followed by a right hook sent the neighbour to the ground. Then the neighbour picked up a long, thick titoki pole and struck Henry very hard across the lower part of his body. The force of the blow broke one of Henry's legs and he fell heavily to the ground on his back. The neighbour jumped on him and tried to gouge out his eyes with his thumbs. Luckily, another settler, passing by to post a letter at the store, came to Henry's assistance.

Hearing the commotion from inside the house, Sarah had come out to investigate and she and the passerby managed to get Henry inside. Sarah's father, Joseph Masters, was sent for and he made a pair of splints for the injured leg with his knife. Henry could not return to work on the road and Sarah nursed him until he could walk again. As often happens in these circumstances, the patient married the nurse, the wedding taking place on May 2 1857. Henry was 42 years of age and Sarah 29. The witnesses on the marriage certificate were Joseph Masters and Sarah Dixon. The officiating minister was the Reverend William Ronaldson of the Church Missionary Society, who had come to visit Sarah and interpreted the Maori speeches when Sarah had first arrived in the district some two years earlier with her four young children and her first husband.

Both Sarah and Henry had been married before. Henry Bannister, born at Sedgley in Staffordshire in 1815, lost his wife during the first year of marriage and had been so saddened by his loss he decided to leave England and go to the Australian gold diggings. He had some success there but he did not make his fortune. He was friendly with a man who had been to 'Pig Island', as New Zealand was sometimes known, and told Henry there was money to be made buying pigs from the Maori and shipping them to Sydney. As pork was very expensive at the diggings, Henry decided to have a go at this trade and in 1842 he set sail for Wellington. Little is known about Henry Bannister for the next 15 years, so I do not know how successful he was in his various business enterprises.

Sarah Bannister (née Masters).

Richard Iorns' will had left the store to Sarah, but it became known as 'Bannister's' and Henry took over the duties of postmaster from his wife. A formed track from Wellington over the Rimutakas was opened in 1856 and this made a great difference to the cost of freight which fell from £20 to £10.10s a ton. Basic items settlers' families had not seen for years started to arrive on the wagon trains and even the mail came twice a week. As Bannister's store was also the post office, it became the meeting place and all the bartering and ordering of goods was done there.

Henry Bannister was a kindly man who offered a helping hand to many new pioneers in the early days. He was involved in many organisations and was often referred to as the 'Father of Masterton', although, of course, Joseph Masters was the 'Founder of Masterton'.

Sarah helped in the store and in the post office but she had her hands full coping with bringing up a large family in poor, cramped conditions. The house had neither a bathroom, laundry nor a toilet and the cooking was done on an open fire in a clay chimney. There was no running water so this had to be collected twice daily from a well. Added to this, she had to contend with fleas, mosquitoes and rats. The Reverend William Ronaldson instructed her in the use of a small hand sewing machine and she became an expert needlewoman, a most useful skill as she had an ever growing family to clothe. Besides the four children – Mary Ann, Joseph, William and Sarah – from her first marriage to Richard Iorns, she had a further three sons, Henry, John and Charles by the end of 1861.

In 1856 money was sought for a school in Masterton and the next year the early settlers contributed a total of £40 in money and goods towards this. The main contributors were Henry Bannister, Charles Dixon, Edward Cheer, Robert Dagg, Bennett Perry, Edward Eaton, Henry Jones and Holmes Crayne, who became the schoolmaster. The building was finished in 1857 and was used as a school, church and town hall.

The settlement of Masterton was now firmly established and had a slowly mounting population. Edward Chittenden, an early pioneer, wrote in the September 19 1860 issue of the *New Zealander Advertiser* : "Our own little village … of 4,000 acres of the best land in New Zealand. 35 actual small farm settlers whose families number about 144 souls." He mentioned the "snug little cottage of Joseph Masters" at the south east end of the village. Going west from Masters' house "a line of cottages and cultivations stretches along for several miles in that direction" to where the great NE road crossed the village. Here there "seems to be the nucleus of a future city. This is Mr Bannister's store".

CHAPTER 6

AUGUSTUS ARRIVES IN MASTERTON

Augustus William Cave was born in the small village of Avening Green, Tortworth in the Cotswolds in 1840, the year the Treaty of Waitangi was signed in New Zealand. Augustus was the eldest child of William Cave and Caroline Mills, who were married in the parish church of Nympsfield, Gloucestershire on May 24 1838. At that time William was residing in the family home, 'Field Farm', just outside the village of Nympsfield.

The Caves had been farmers for many years. The census return of 1851 showed the farm at Tortworth, run by William Cave, was 180 acres, and 'Field Farm', in the charge of his brother John, consisted of 146 acres.

The next child born to William and Caroline was Mary Elizabeth, who was my maternal great-grandmother. After this birth, Caroline had a further seven children, three daughters and four sons.

Augustus' paternal grandfather was Thomas Cave, who

Nympsfield church.

died at the age of 89 at Nympsfield on June 24 1847. A local newspaper cutting stated: "He was a kind father and an affectionate husband. He served the office of church warden for the parish of Nympsfield under three ministers for fifty successive years and was tenant under three Lord Ducies in the same parish for upwards of sixty years." Sheep were the principal animals kept on his farm, the wool industry being very important in England in the 17th and 18th centuries.

Thomas Cave was born in 1758 and he married Mary Collins on April 8 1788 at Nympsfield Parish Church. The wedding notice of March 22 1788 stated that Thomas Cave was a bachelor in the parish of Nympsfield and a pig killer by occupation. Mary Cave had four children but, sadly, she died on April 29 1798, aged only 37. When Thomas Cave married Elizabeth Deane on March 30 1802, the wedding notice now described Thomas Cave as a yeoman. Elizabeth Cave had four sons, one of whom was William Cave, and one daughter.

In 1823 Thomas Cave was involved in setting up 'The Nympsfield Club', a charity for the benefit of the poor in the parish of Nympsfield and he was one of the signatories to the document. I gather this charity is still in existence today.

Going back a generation, I was lucky enough to find the will of Thomas Cave of Owlpen, drawn up on April 9 1778. He was born on June 3 1722 and he died on April 22 1778, aged 55. He married Sarah Gingell on July 14 1750 and they had 12 children, one of whom was Thomas Cave, the father of William Cave. In his will he left property in Owlpen, Uley and Avening and described his occupation as 'broadweaver'.

Owlpen church.

Cloth manufacture was the first industry to develop around Stroud, the hills ideal for grazing sheep for wool. The surrounding valleys, with their rapid streams, provided an abundant supply of water needed to process the wool into cloth. By the mid 1500s fulling mills were widespread around Stroud.

On further investigation, I discovered that many men and women in the Cam valley, which includes Dursley, Uley and Owlpen worked in the numerous mills, while even more worked at home producing the famous West of England broadcloth with its world-wide reputation.

The area around Stroud produced the famous Stroud Scarlet broadcloth, used to clothe England's redcoat soldiers. Stroud Scarlet became a very famous colour and was in great demand for soldiers' uniforms.

The yarn was prepared in the mills with weavers collecting the yarn and weaving it on a loom at home. Broadcloth weaving needed two persons, one to throw and one to catch the shuttle, because of the width involved. It was called double handed weaving. The shuttle was thrown across the loom by the weaver at the right hand side and caught in the left hand by the other weaver so the shuttle, in this old fashioned way, was continuously thrown from one person to the other. The term broadloom still applies to some fabrics such as carpets.

Weaving was often a family affair as the children did some of the work. The master weavers, rather respectable men, kept from four to six looms in their homes.

From the Middle Ages onwards, production of wool and then the manufacture of cloth dominated the Cotswolds until the 1830s when increased competition from abroad and from the North of England, and the public taste for worsteds brought about the decline in the cloth trade in this part of the country.

Thomas Cave of Owlpen's father was also Thomas Cave. He was born on February 1 1685 and on July 10 1709 he married Elizabeth Butcher. They had six children and Thomas died in 1740 aged 54. His father, Lionel Cave of Owlpen, was born in 1657, fathered nine children with Jane and died aged 72 in 1729.

His father, another Lionel, is mentioned in documents

dated July 20 1662 and January 14 1663 regarding the equipping and arming of the Owlpen Light Horse Militia. Lionel's father may have witnessed or even taken part in the Civil War.

There is a reference to a Lyonel Cave in the Owlpen Manor Papers: "Lyonel Cave has returned from visiting his mother in deepest Somerset". This was the earliest reference to the Caves that I have found.

It has been quite an achievement, I feel, managing to go back nine generations to the English Civil War.

Augustus William Cave was educated at Dursley Grammar School, somewhat unusual for a farmer's son in those days. Then, in 1862, when he was 22, he decided he would like to make a new life in the 'Colonies' and he set sail from England for New Zealand in the ship *Maria*. The passage at that time was very unpleasant and hazardous and took about three months.

It is interesting to note that at this time emigration to Australia was positively encouraged with cheap passages offered by landlords, workhouses, and central government. Pioneers were also given the opportunity of acquiring land on which to raise sheep. This was particularly attractive to people from the Cotswolds who had been raised in this industry and who could see the possibilities of a new woollen trade developing in Australia. In fact, the scheme was so popular the population of Australia rose from 437,665 in 1851 to three million by 1889.

Having survived the voyage, Augustus recuperated in Wellington for a period. One day he read in a Wellington paper about the Small Farms' Association in Masterton and the wonderful opportunities that existed there. After some deliberation, he decided to visit Masterton and have a look for himself. As he did not have the funds to buy land he decided to engage in the carrying trade to build up a sufficient deposit for a farm.

For the first few years he was employed as a driver conveying goods between Masterton and Wellington. In the beginning bullocks were used as the pack animals but the ground over the Rimutakas was too hard for their hooves and they soon developed foot problems. Later on, draught horses were shipped in from Australia and they were much better suited for pulling wagons.

It was a tough life for a driver, as the roads and bridges were very primitive and there were many accidents on the Rimutakas. The track over the ranges was very narrow and there were few places where two vehicles could pass each other. Sometimes stagecoaches were blown over or became stuck in the snow. Crossing rivers was extremely hazardous and they took their toll. Out of the first 12 people buried in the Masterton cemetery, four were drowned. With the lack of work in Wellington, many tried the job of wagon or coach driver, but most soon gave up this arduous occupation.

Besides being tough, the journey to and from Wellington was also very time consuming. Augustus would leave Masterton at daybreak on Monday morning and return late on Friday night. He would unload on Saturday morning and then load up the wagon in the afternoon ready for the journey again on Monday morning. The goods he took to Wellington were mainly wool, sheep skins, hides, bacon and salt butter in large kegs.

In 1866 Augustus started a carrying company in partnership with Henry Bannister. As well as travelling to and from Wellington, they delivered goods to the outlying sheep stations. They became so busy they needed three wagon teams, with 12 animals in each team. The partnership brought the freight charge down to £10.10s per ton and then to £6.10s per ton, where it remained for many years. It should be noted that the wagon trade, until the opening of the rail link to Featherston in 1878, was one of the most important businesses in the Wairarapa.

One day while feeding his horses at Upper Hutt, Augustus noticed a number of sparrows hopping about. This scene reminded him very much of his younger days, when he helped his father on his farm in the English Cotswolds so he decided he would like to bring them back to Masterton. He obtained a box, put some young sparrows inside and fed them when he arrived home. After a short while he released them and they multiplied very quickly. In a few years there were many sparrows around his home in Masterton and this pleased him greatly although, unfortunately, they did become a pest to some of the small farmers.

During the eight years he was engaged in the carrying

trade, Augustus had many accidents of a minor nature. Others were more major and on one occasion one of his horses drowned. But it was the serious accident he had at Abbotts Bridge, just outside Featherston, which dramatically changed his life. Men working on the bridge warned him it was not safe, but unfortunately he took no notice. When he was in the middle of the bridge, it collapsed. He fell 20-30 feet onto the rocks below. Three of his horses were killed instantly and another had to be shot. He became very deaf as a result of this accident. The whole incident upset him a great deal and he decided to give up driving and to concentrate on farming.

While Augustus was a wagon train driver, Masterton started to expand, although not as fast as Greytown. In May 1863 the first licensed hotel – the 'Family Hotel' – opened in Masterton, with John Tuck the proprietor. It was later renamed the 'Prince of Wales'. In 1864 the first Anglican church was built. The Reverend William Ronaldson was appointed the first resident minister and personally built the first vicarage in Church Street.

Duncan McGregor.

About 1865, the Te Ore Ore Maori came out in sympathy with the turbulent natives of Taranaki and Waikato. They started to march and parade through the streets of Masterton in large numbers brandishing muskets, spears and tomahawks. The local settlers were very careful not to provoke them, but decided to form a volunteer force in Greytown at the 'British Volunteer Hotel'. The government equipped them with arms and ammunition and also sent a drill instructor to instill some discipline. About 200 friendly Maori from Manaia and Akura came and camped in Masterton to protect the residents. The appearance of these Maori, together with the establishment of the volunteer force, had the desired effect of calming the situation and no further threatening demonstrations occurred.

However, the government believed there could be some disagreement with Maori in the future and erected a stockade for the use of settlers in 1868, in case of an attack. It was garrisoned by eight armed men who each night raised the drawbridge over the moat by block and tackle. After a few months, the situation cooled and the garrison was discharged.

In 1871 the first Agricultural Show was held in what was to become Masterton Park and it was a great success with good showings of cattle, sheep and horses. In the same year, the first Masterton race meeting was held. Prizes such as saddles and bridles were awarded and the chief winner was a Maori horse named Poto Poto. During the next few years race meetings were held on William Donald's property at Manaia.

An 1869 survey of buildings in Masterton listed the dwellings in Bridge Street – with many streams crossing it – and later named Queen Street. Starting at the Waipoua River crossing and going south, the first house on the left-hand side was Robert Hare's store; then came St. Matthew's Church; a building erected by Duncan McGregor and used as a Sunday School; then Farquhar Gray's blacksmith's shop; and next came the stables of Bannister and Cave's Carrying Company. In front of the stables there was a pump and watering trough and behind it a large lean-to. This was used to store corn, but when empty was used for functions such as volunteer dinners and harvest suppers. After the stables came the 'Prince of Wales' and then Augustus' cottage. Next was Walter Perry's butcher's shop; then the Scottish church; William Greathead's blacksmith's shop; Alfred Renall's mill, a very distinctive landmark; and, finally, Michael Dixon's house at Kuripuni.

CHAPTER 7

AUGUSTUS AND MASTERTON THRIVE

On April 14 1869 Augustus William Cave married Mary Ann Iorns, the stepdaughter of his partner, Henry Bannister, and granddaughter of Joseph Masters. Mary Ann, affectionately known throughout most of her life as 'Polly', was the young girl who 14 years earlier and only seven years old had trekked across the Rimutakas with her father and mother when they first made the exhausting journey to Masterton.

On December 17 1869 Augustus purchased 100 acres of land described as 'Te Ahitanga' No. 2 Block, for £250 from the Maori chief Wi Tinitara Te Kaewa and other "Aboriginal Natives" and on October 17 1872, purchased a further 143 acres for £357 from the same block of land and the

Mary Ann 'Polly' Cave.

same Maori chief. He then began building a farmhouse called 'Woodleigh' which turned out to be "a charming residence" according to *The Cyclopedia of New Zealand*. The land he purchased at Te Ore Ore was some years later bisected by Soldiers Settlement Road.

On July 16 1870 there was much sadness when Mary Ann's mother, Sarah Bourton, died at only 42, just a few months after giving birth to the eighth Bannister baby, Thomas, on January 26. In all, Sarah had four children with Richard Iorns and eight more with Henry Bannister. After the birth, Sarah, who had never visited a doctor in her life, suffered terrible toothache and a medical man was summoned from Greytown. He pulled out the offending tooth but complications set in and she died within three days. As Mary Ann sat by the side of her dying mother, she promised to take care of the new baby. This she did, besides looking after the next youngest child, a two-year-old girl. In fact there always seemed to be some family member living under her wing at 'Woodleigh' and her own sister, Sarah Iorns, also lived there until she was married at the age of 31.

Later in the same year, Mary Ann had a baby boy of her own who was named William Henry.

Apart from building the house, Augustus had to clear the bush on his property and there are several advertisements in the *Wairarapa Daily Times* calling for tenders to do the work. He started to buy sheep principally for their wool and he also bred cattle. He was also very good at ploughing with bullocks – the first large-scale ploughing in the district was done by a Mr Harding and Augustus when they ploughed 20 acres, ready for sowing with wheat. However, Augustus' main interest and passion was horses. He started training racehorses for their owners and built his own private training track at 'Woodleigh' for this purpose. He then progressed on to breeding racehorses and Clydesdales.

There was an interesting advertisement in the *Wairarapa Daily Times* on August 19 1893 which stated:

"Mr A W Cave of Te Ore Ore has added materially to the draught stock of the district by the importation from Southland of the draught Clydesdale stallion, 'The MacGregor'. The pedigree of this animal will bear favourable comparison with that of any sire in the district. 'The MacGregor' will stand this season at Mr Cave's farm Te Ore Ore."

Masterton was still growing more slowly than Greytown or Featherston, in part because of the greater distance from Wellington. In 1874 Masterton was still very much a pioneer settlement. Richard Brown, who moved there that year, recorded the following description of the town.

"In 1874, it was a bush township at an early stage of development. Much of the adjacent plain was still under Totara [a native New Zealand tree] and other forest and in places clumps of bush extended to the main street. A bridge was constructed at about that time over the Waiohine, but none of the rivers were bridged in Masterton or its near neighbourhood. The roads, formed by digging a ditch on either side and casting the spoil inward, were a morass of mud in winter and very dusty in summer. For many years afterwards, stumps left in the roads continued to give a great deal of trouble when excavation work was in hand. Many of the houses when I arrived were built of milled timber, but there were a number of others constructed of pit sawn slabs. Bullock teams were relied upon for the heavy traction of that day, though carts and lighter vehicles were also in use."

In 1872 Augustus, with James McKillop and and a Mr Gillies, drove three covered wagons to bring Scandinavian immigrants from Wellington to Masterton. The men walked and the women and children rode in the wagons. On their arrival in Masterton, they were lodged in the stockade. They then moved north and started to fell the area called the Forty Mile Bush; they were also employed in road making. They were very efficient at this and the majority of them proved to be very good pioneers. They settled in places such as Mauriceville and Eketahuna.

In September 1874, the Bank of New Zealand opened a branch in Masterton and there was much general building work. As a consequence, property values soared. Another important event was the opening of the Ruamahunga River bridge at Te Ore Ore for traffic, by the superintendent of the Wellington Provincial District, the Honourable Sir William Fitzherbert, on January 14 1875.

In March 1875, after a great deal of effort from certain individuals, the first resident doctor arrived in Masterton. A Cornishman, Dr William Hosking had arrived in New Zealand in 1863 and first practised at Bluff, then at Hokitika and finally at the Ross goldfields. Also in March 1875, a proposal to form a Masterton Town Board led to the beginning of local government when the first meeting was held at the School House in Dixon Street on August 26. In July that year the first resident solicitor, Mr C F Gawith, arrived in town.

The next year, 1876, was a very sad one for the Caves because on May 24 their only child, William Henry, died at only six years old. The death certificate stated he had been sickly from birth. Mary Ann had no more children.

Also in 1876 the first Fire Brigade began operating and was in considerable demand because of the many wooden buildings in Masterton.

Now the population of Masterton was increasing rapidly and, at a meeting on March 23 1877, it was decided to petition for the settlement to become a borough, as its increased numbers now entitled it to. The new borough, with considerably enhanced boundaries covering 4,311 acres, was proclaimed on July 10. The mayoral election was set for July 28 and Robert George Williams became the first mayor of Masterton. Many citizens wanted Henry Bannister to stand but he declined the honour because of his failing health. However, he was persuaded to become a town councillor and he attended a few meetings before he finally retired to his farm at Opaki, named 'Sedgley' after his home town in England.

In 1877 the first Masterton Hospital was established on land facing Te Ore Ore Road. Augustus made several large donations towards costs.

The 1878 census showed Masterton's population had now leapfrogged the other towns in the area to an impressive 1,673 – one-fifth of the Wairarapa's 8,263 residents now lived in the Masterton area. This much increased population was reflected in land values. In 1870 it was almost impossible to find a buyer for any unsold Masterton town plots but by 1875 they were selling for £130 to £200 and Masterton had by then taken over the mantle of being the principal Wairarapa town.

On July 21 1878 Augustus doubled the size of his farm when he purchased the 270 acres of land named 'Rangitumau Block sections 65, 66 and 67' for £675 from McRae Drummond. This land was at the end of what was later named Caves Road after Augustus. This name remains today, as do most of the other road names in Masterton honouring the early pioneers.

There was more sadness for the Caves in 1879 when, in June, Henry Bannister, Augustus' former partner and stepfather-in-law, died after a lingering illness. He was a kindly, happy, genial man who had helped many people over the years, so it was not surprising friends came to his funeral from all parts of the Wairarapa and the townsfolk turned out in great numbers. The funeral cortege, consisting of gigs, traps and buggies, was so long it reached from the Waipoua Bridge up to and beyond the Terrace. Then in October, Augustus' mother, Caroline, died at the age of 59. It was very sad to think that Augustus had not seen or even spoken to his mother since he left for New Zealand some 17 years earlier. In those days when one set sail for the bottom of the world, a person knew in his, or her, heart it was very unlikely he or she would ever see their relatives in England again. The goodbyes on the quayside must have been very emotional and heartbreaking.

At the end of the decade, after farming for 10 years, Augustus had substantially increased his flock of sheep and in consequence greatly increased his income. It is interesting to note that wool exports in the Wellington province were only £2,500 in 1846, increased to £47,000 in 1853, £125,000 in 1861, £208,000 in 1871 and to £624,000 in 1876.

On November 1 1880, the rail link to Masterton was opened. The first train from Wellington to Masterton was one and a half hours late, but the crowd remained enthusiastic and there was a fine celebration dinner with many speeches. The wagon trade had been the only way to take goods over the Rimutakas for many years, but now the railway became the main transporter of goods and provisions. The arrival of the railway resulted in considerable growth in the town and a large number of new businesses were opened. However, the cost of rail transport was high, particularly for horses in horse boxes. Augustus attended a meeting held at the Masterton 'Club Hotel' to consider the charges. He emphasised that the cost of conveying horses was too high and it was decided a deputation would wait on the Railway Commissioners. This resulted in the lowering of the charges for horse boxes.

Between 1874 and 1884 there were three big floods in the Wairarapa. The first was in 1874, the second in 1881 and the third on September 1 1884. As far as Augustus was concerned, the second in March 1881 was the worst. Te Ore Ore was one sheet of water except for some islets on which sheep were crowded. A lot of Augustus' land was under water and he lost some stock.

CHAPTER 8
CAVE THE FARMER

Augustus had every reason to remember 1885, the year his father, William Cave, decided to emigrate to New Zealand and spend his last few years with his eldest son. William's wife Caroline had died six years earlier and the desire to see his son after 23 years must have been very great. It was certainly remarkable, and courageous to attempt the hazardous voyage at the ripe old age of 78. The conditions on board the sailing ships were primitive, and frequent deaths occurred from the various perils ranging from disease to shipwrecks.

William Cave survived the voyage and the meeting with his son on the quayside at Wellington would have been an emotional moment. During the next few months, William would have spent many hours recounting to his son stories about his brothers and sisters and farming life in the Cotswolds. In return, Augustus would have shown his father how Masterton had progressed from a small settlement to a prosperous town and how his farm had grown from an area of bush to a highly successful enterprise. In fact *The Cyclopedia of New Zealand* stated that "Mr Cave's farm may be considered a model one". The entry went on to say that in 1895 his flock consisted of 1,200 Lincoln sheep and he also had about 100 head of cattle. It is interesting to note that by 1886 the population of Masterton had nearly doubled to 3,160 from the 1,673 recorded only eight years previously. Possibly as a consequence of this, the first gas main was laid in 1888.

On June 15 1888, Augustus bought 222 acres of land titled the 'Taueru' Section 23 for £1,776 from F G Moore. This land was next to the 'Te Ahitanga' Block, purchased by Augustus in 1869 and 1872 on the other side of the Wangaehu River. Then on December 23 1895 he purchased a further 122

Above: William Cave, Christopher Pope's great-great-grandfather.
Below: His wife, Caroline Cave (née Mills).

acres in the 'Te Ahitanga' Block. This brought Augustus' total land holding up to 857 acres – 365 acres in the 'Te Ahitanga' Block, 222 acres in the 'Taueru' Section and 270 acres in the 'Rangitumau' Block.

On October 17 1888, the following article appeared in the *Wairarapa Daily Times* about a visit to Augustus Cave's farm.

"A Te Ore Ore Farm

"It was our good fortune yesterday to be invited to visit a typical farm in this neighbourhood, which, though it may not claim to be the very model of a modern pattern farm, is in fertility and resources an admirable example of those properties which have the honour of supporting the population of this Britain of the South, and of paying the lion's share of all rates and taxes. In Wairarapa North, there are, we know, and we are grateful to acknowledge the fact, many substantial farms which are highly productive – few more so, perhaps, than the one we visited yesterday, belonging to Mr A W Cave.

"This farm contains some six hundred acres of

Mary Ann and Augustus Cave at 'Woodleigh'.

level land with a ring fence, and if anyone deems a six hundred acre estate a small affair, he has not, like us, walked round it, and learned to treat such a block with the consideration which it deserves. This particular area of level plain stretches from the low Te Ore Ore hills on its western boundary for a couple of miles or so towards the higher elevation at Otahuao, and appears to be about a mile in width. In the centre of this plain, one gets a sense of space and room, of fresh air and extended horizon, which cannot be realized in the adjacent town. The deep but sluggish Wangaehu River running in a southerly direction divides the farm into two sections. Between this stream and the Te Ore Ore hills is the rich agricultural land; beyond the river to the east is the fine grazing land, which is one of the marked features of the estate. In the latter part more especially there are bush clearings and bush paddocks which contrast with the almost bowling green surface of the land west of the Wangaehu. "The homestead itself is very centrally situated;

Stacking hay at 'Woodleigh' with Augustus Cave at top of ladder.

a sort of oasis amongst the big grain and grass paddocks. A commodious two-storey residence is framed with a pleasant garden, and bordered with a circle of shade and shelter trees. Just outside, there are outbuildings, yards, and other appurtenances essential to the working of a large farm. The garden deserves special notice because it is a little ahead of most gardens in the district, and illustrates what an amateur who puts heart into his work can accomplish. This garden is tended by Mr Cave's father, with whom horticulture is evidently a labour of love. We were a little surprised to find in what might be regarded as an out-of-the-way spot, an unknown garden, tall rows of peas in pod, big cabbages with solid hearts, new potatoes, the size of hen's eggs, (we brought a sample away for the inspection of the incredulous), and ripe strawberries. We might also dilate on well-trained fruit trees, a good greenhouse, and skilfully trimmed shrubs, did our space permit; but it was quite evident that if Mr Cave, senior, well advanced in years as he is, were to take it into his head to prepare exhibits for the Masterton Horticultural Show he would make many of our younger gardeners take a second place.

"Turning back once more to the farm, we are reminded by the fields of young wheat that we are

Mary Ann and Augustus Cave on 'Woodleigh' farm in 1904.

on the celebrated Te Ore Ore soil which year after year produces big harvests of grain without sign of exhaustion or deterioration. The land is essentially wheat land, of a quality to gladden the heart of a farmer, and this season Mr Cave is devoting a hundred and sixty acres of it to the crop for which it is so specially adapted. Other crops, however, are not overlooked, at least a hundred acres being reserved for turnips. If we inspect the grazing parts of the estate, we find that Mr Cave runs a hundred head of cattle, between one and two thousand sheep, and horses enough to stock half a dozen racecourses. There is, however, belonging to the same proprietor other grazing ground some three miles further north on the Wangaehu hills, which is also valuable for its excellent pasturage; but on the farm proper there is now a wealth of grass which defies the efforts of the stock to keep it down.

"The stock, too, we must not forget to mention, is as good as the land, the cattle being well graded shapely beasts, the sheep carrying big fleeces, and the horses of the sort over which racing men rave. The farm is now a stud farm, with the superb Piscatorious as monarch, and at his court are many of the titled equine demoiselles in our Turf Guide. In his loose box, at home on Te Ore Ore, Piscatorious, with his shapely form, strong quarters, beautiful head, and satin skin, appears to be almost a marvel. Wandering through the paddocks where the mares graze and the foals romp, we have a confused recollection of being introduced to Traducers, Tim Whifflers, Riddlesworths, and other highly related quadrupeds, but as we could not tell one from the other, we will not pretend to individualise the assemblage of blood, bone, and beauty which is now gathered at the court of King Piscatorious.

"We spent several pleasant hours about the farm and congratulated ourselves upon the possession in this district of fertile and productive properties of such a character. After viewing carefully the valuable estate, the product of fourteen years enterprise and industry on the part of Mr A W Cave, we left with a stronger belief than ever in the resources of this district. Farms like this are the mainstay of the colony and farmers like Mr Cave are its backbone."

Augustus and Mary Ann often helped out the various members of the Iorns and Bannister families. In August 1892 Richard Bannister stayed at 'Woodleigh' for some time when he was very ill with pleurisy. On December 11 1895 the reception of the wedding of Charles Bannister to Miss Agnes McKenzie was held at 'Woodleigh' and Augustus gave the bride away in the Frank Johnstone-Phebe Bannister wedding.

By 1896 the population of Masterton had grown to nearly 3,500 and it was still increasing steadily. The town had spread out and now substantial homes, particularly in Queen Street, were being built of brick to replace their wooden predecessors.

Sadly, William Cave died on December 13 1896. He had been laid low with influenza 12 months previously and never really regained his health. He had lived another 11 years after arriving in New Zealand at the age of 78 and had led a very active life, until the very last year. He was a very keen gardener and it was said few gardens in the district could equal his. He was a man of singularly amiable disposition and his passing was mourned by many people. There were many wreaths and floral tributes at his funeral, including one from the Masterton Racing Club. As has already been described, when his coffin was being lowered into the grave, Katerina Wi Waka, a well-known Maori woman, placed a large rug over it as a mark of deep sympathy.

Several interesting articles appeared in the *Wairarapa Daily Times* about various incidents at 'Woodleigh Farm'. One stated: "A rumour has been published that Mr A W Cave lost hundreds of acres of wheat. Mr Cave informed us that he lost no wheat, as it was all safely harvested before the late rain." In another: "During the last few days a fire has been running at Te Ore Ore on the property of Mr A W Cave, which has destroyed about 100 acres of grass

Augustus Cave, on the left, at 'Woodleigh' with a threshing mill in the background.

and a considerable stretch of fencing. Last night's rain has checked it, but the logs in the bush portion of the land are still alight." There was a notice about trespass: "Any person found trespassing on the properties of the undersigned at Te Ore Ore and Wangaehu with dog or gun will be prosecuted. A W Cave, J P Perry, H James, G Drummond, W Iorns, T F Shaw, Cameron brothers, D McKenzie, J Morrison." Another article noted 'Woodleigh' was a receiving depot for goods to be sold in aid of the Boer War effort. Another item mentioned that Mrs Cave had promised to present a gold-mounted riding whip to the winner of the Bracelet Race at the Masterton Races. In her prizegiving speech, she said that, although her horse 'Woodleigh' had come second, she was not disappointed since a woman owned the winning horse.

Around 1881, Charles Bannister was sent by Augustus to move 900 sheep from Alfredton to 'Woodleigh' and his account of the sheep drive, in his book *Early History of the Wairarapa*, is well worth quoting from.

> "I was sent by Mr A W Cave to lift 900 four-tooth store wethers from Holmes Warren's Tiraumea Station. I had for my mate the late Woody Livingston. We arrived there in time for tea. We were treated well on this station. The sheep were ready for us and the head shepherd had a long tailed two tooth in the mob for dog food. The cook gave our dogs a good feed that night and we shut them up in the stable.

I noticed about a dozen dogs tied to their kennels. In the middle of the night we were awakened with a whip cracking and a row with two men swearing at one another. It turned out that the shepherd's dogs and the rabbiter's dogs had been barking most of the night and the bullock driver had got his whip which he kept handy and was giving them a taste of it.

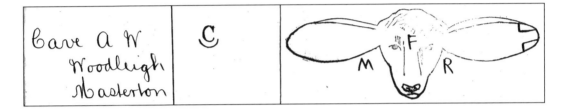

Sheep identification, 'Woodleigh', Masterton.

"The bullocky was at the dog kennels in his pyjamas and the second shepherd was on the verandah, saying what he was going to do to the bullocky. The bullocky rushed at the shepherd cracking his whip and saying, 'What's good for his dog is good for its master if he keeps on barking'. The shepherd went into his room and locked the door. We left there next morning at daylight and got to George's Alfredton Hotel in good time. I only had to ride in front of those big hardy wethers. The next day we made Tikitapu Station. The following day we arrived at Woodleigh in time for afternoon tea and counted our sheep. We killed a sheep for the dogs giving them the inside. Our dogs got some of the long tailer and so did we. Some of the old time drovers well remember Woody Livingston's old yellow dog. He was the best dog I had ever seen on the side of a big mob of sheep."

CHAPTER 9

CAVE AND THE COMMUNITY

One of Augustus' main interests was the Masterton Agricultural and Pastoral Association. He took a prominent part in its formation and also successfully helped to bring it through difficulties in the early years.

In 1870 Henry Bannister, with some farmers, formed the Wairarapa Pastoral and Agricultural Society and a show was held in the Masterton Stockade. When, on August 20 1878, the Wairarapa East Coast Pastoral and Agricultural Association was registered, it was the genuine hope of many individuals there would be just one show association in the Wairarapa. Unfortunately this did not happen so, in 1885, a meeting was held and the Masterton A & P Association was formed. On November 25 1885, the first annual show of this association was held in the sale yards of Messrs Lowes and Iorns in Renall Street. Augustus with John McKenzie, David Guild and William Iorns were the cattle stewards.

At this show there was a shearing match, each competitor having 20 minutes to shear three sheep. Only one competitor, H Wilton, finished within the time limit and he was declared the winner. This led to other competitions for local entrants in the following years and it was subsequently decided to hold an event open to all comers which eventually became the Golden Shears International Shearing Championship.

In the minutes of the 1885 annual show, A W Cave was shown to be one of the members of the general committee. At the Masterton A & P Association's annual meeting of 1891, William Lowes retired from the position of president and was succeeded by Augustus. At this meeting it was decided to start an industrial section at the next show. In March 1892 the Association purchased 20 acres in Dixon Street for a new showground, but funds were stretched with this purchase. There was a note in the *Wairarapa Daily Times* on March 3 1892, saying that Augustus had been canvassing for the Association and had managed to find 35 new members. At the Annual Meeting on June 8 1892, Farquar Gray was elected president and on June 21 the Association was finally incorporated. Augustus was elected president again at the AGM of 1893 and re-elected the following year.

The decision was made on December 8 1897 to build a grandstand for the show in February the next year and it was completed just in time. In June 1899, it was decided a monthly paper should be printed covering various agricultural matters and it should be distributed to all members. Despite some difficulties in previous years, the 19th century drew to a close with the Masterton A & P Association in a good financial position.

The first two-day show, held in February 1902, was an outstanding success. There were 701 entries in the sheep class, while total stock entries were 1,435, a record for the colony. The Association now had wide support. The 1900 membership was 284, two years later it reached 625 and by mid 1904, it had increased to an impressive total of 800 names. The Masterton A & P Association was now truly launched on its long history.

Some time during the next few years, Augustus was appointed patron of the Association and he was finally given the distinction of being made an honorary life member in recognition of his long and distinguished service.

Augustus Cave examining flock.

At the 1892 Show, Augustus exhibited the champion bullock and also won the guessing competition for the weight of a bullock – all 948 lbs. Augustus and Charles Cockburn-Hood each guessed 950 lbs and R J Dagg came next with 945 lbs. Interestingly, the weights guessed ranged from 675 lbs to 1,100 lbs. As Augustus was a highly respected member of the local farming community, he was asked to judge various animal classes at different shows, particularly draught horses. In July 1895, for example, he judged the draughts at the Hawke's Bay Agricultural Society Show.

Augustus Cave was also for many years a director of the Wairarapa Farmers' Co-operative Association and, in 1899, a promoter of the new Masterton Farmers' Implement Company. In 1895 he wrote a testimonial for D Hartley's Hogget Drench!

Racehorses were his other passion and Augustus served on the committees of a variety of racing clubs. He was for many years the president of the Masterton Racing Club.

The first race meeting, held in Masterton in about 1866, was run on a course from the Anglican Church to Jeans' Estate and then on to part of Dixon's Farm. For the next few years, race meetings were held on William Donald's property at Manaia. The next venue was 'Willow Park', William Welch's farm. After the present club was formed in 1876, 127 acres of freehold land was obtained from R Campbell and this became the Masterton Racing Club's permanent home.

An evocative account of an event in 1876 is told by Charles Bannister in his interesting book *Early History of the Wairarapa*, published in 1940. It is of a trip to the races in which both Charles Bannister and Augustus took part, and I have included the full story.

"A party was made up at the Club Hotel for the Wairarapa Races, to be taken in one of Hastwell, Bannister and Cave's large brakes that were used in the transport of goods between Wellington and Masterton. Mr A W Cave was asked to take the whip and reins and to select a good team from the numerous horses used by the company. Seats were made along the sides of the vehicle. These were made cosy with cushions and rugs. Lunch hampers and cases of drinks made up the luggage. We left the Club Hotel at half past eight on a fine morning and arrived at Mr Hastwell's in time for morning tea, which was greatly appreciated after a morning's drive across the Taratahi Plains and through the Three Mile Bush, as Carterton was termed then. After our horses had finished munching their corn and had a drink, they were harnessed up by that old time trainer of Volunteer, Alec Cameron. We started for Tauherenikau, accompanied by a large party from Hastwell's. In due time we arrived at the course. The horses were unhitched and made safe. The old Tauherenikau Grandstand was then in a different position from today. It was on the left of the entrance gate. One thing that I can remember well was that Jack Girdlestone, a member of our party, rode 'Old Libeller'. Girdy, as we called him, had long black whiskers well down to his waist, which when he rode past the winning post well in the lead, were flowing past his ears. Another instance was the antics of that bad tempered horse 'Nanakia' (a very appropriate name). He was coming down the straight well in the lead. About two chains from the winning post a dog crossed the track in front of him. 'Nanakia' stuck his toes in the turf and stopped dead and nothing could shift him. His rider used the whip and spurs in vain. He had to be led off the track. A good many of the betters who had money on him would have liked to have shot him. It was explained he was a pet foal and only went when he liked. In the Produce Stakes the rules were three starters or no second money. Mr T McCarthy of Masterton had entered two horses. But a week before the races one of them died. He was a black bobtailed horse called 'Satan'. He kept the death of his horse a secret and borrowed a black bobtailed horse from my brother Harry. This horse was only beaten by a short head. He got away with second money. The next best thing was lunch in that piece of bush. The good things that were packed in the hampers and boxes, supplemented by Hastwell's contributions, provided a spread that one reads about but never sees now. That evening we returned to Greytown and stayed the night at Hastwell's and spent a glorious time. Up in the morning not too early, some felt like having a good breakfast but some didn't. We enjoyed another good day, but as we left for home up came one of Wairarapa's 'southerly busters'. By the time we got over the Moroa Plain we were wet and cold, but good Jack Edmondson of Edmondson Sellar and Iorns, came to the rescue with a grey blanket each, which was very acceptable. Hastwell wanted us to stop to tea, but our very capable driver shook his head. He was thinking about his horses. We got home safe and sound."

By the end of 1880, Augustus had bred several good racehorses including 'Lady Grey' and 'Queen Coil'. He was subsequently very successful as a racehorse breeder and owner. He bred, owned and raced 'Sea Serpent', 'Seal', 'On Dit', 'Rose Fisher', 'First King' and 'Katofeldto.' The mother of these six well-known racehorses was 'Rumour'. As has already been mentioned, it was recorded that at the local race meetings, Mr Cave's colours had often forged their way to the front and the wins had always been popular with the locals. Presumably this was because many local people bet on his horses to win. Augustus Cave's registered racing colours were canary, black sleeve, canary and black cap. Augustus' splendid private training track at 'Woodleigh' was obviously used by his racehorses to great advantage to prepare for their races!

Wairarapa Daily Times advertisement, August 1894.

Piscatorious

WILL stand this season, at his owner's farm, Te Ore Ore. Piscatorious by Traducer (imported) out of Fanny Fisher by Fisherman (imported). Terms £4 4s per mare. For particulars apply to the undersigned.

Randwick,

WILL also stand this season, at his owner s farm. Randwick is by Barbarian, dam Gipsy Girl. For extended pedigree see Victorian Stud Book. Colour a golden chestnut ; stands 15 hands 3 inches in height, and is of immense power and blood ; his sire being full brother to " The Barb," the best horse of the day in New South Wales, by the famed Sir Hercules. Terms £4 4s.

THE Clydesdale Stallion

McGregor

Will stand this season at his owners farm, Te Ore Ore. Full particulars and pedigree apply to

A. W. CAVE, Te Ore Ore.

'Randwick' was another of Augustus' racehorses. The *Wairarapa Daily Times* reported: "Randwick had strains of the best blood that has yet raced in the Australasian Colonies, being by the Barbarian, a son of Sir Hercules". 'Randwick' had an excellent record as a racehorse and was never particular about the weight he carried, or what distance he had to travel, because if he was fit and well, he generally won. He was a golden bright bay chestnut standing at 15 hands 3 inches and was a stylish horse with plenty of bone and muscle.

'Piscatorious' by 'Traducer' out of 'Fanny Fisher' belonged to Augustus and was another good performer on the track. "He had some superb wins and his record would equal anything in the district at that time," claimed the *Wairarapa Daily Times.* Augustus placed an advertisement in the local paper on August 21 1894 advising that his racehorses 'Piscatorious' and 'Randwick' would stand at 'Woodleigh' for the season and the fee for a mare mating with either horse was £4.4s.

The 1890 committee of Masterton A&P Association. Augustus Cave, second from left, front row.

For several years, Augustus was elected the president of the Masterton Opaki Racing Club, and on October 31 1892 he was elected president of the Wairarapa Racing

Club, which held their races at Tauherenikau. This was a beautiful location and race meetings there became important events in the Wairarapa social calendar.

With his passion for horses, hunting was another of Augustus' interests. An article in the *Wairarapa Daily Times* in 1895 reported:

> "Quite a large number of people went out to Te Ore Ore yesterday to watch the hunt over Mr A W Cave's property. About twenty five members followed the hounds, including one lady – Miss Cotter, who, mounted on 'Syringa', rode pluckily and with good judgment. Once, at an awkward jump, the lady lost her stirrup, but did not lose her seat and making a fine recovery, took the remaining fences at a gallop to make up lost ground very rapidly. Mr. Tully, Master of the Hounds, was present and huntsman Welch had charge of the pack. Huntsmen and visitors were most hospitably entertained by Mr Cave, who provided a splendid luncheon for all present. Pressure on our space prevents a more detailed account, but altogether yesterday's run at Te Ore Ore must be considered one of the most enjoyable this season. A few spills occurred, but no-one was injured."

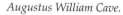

Augustus William Cave.

Besides racing and hunting, Augustus took a keen interest in field sports of all kinds and in 1900 was appointed president of the Wangaehu Rifle Club. He was also president of the Masterton Rugby Football Club for many years. In 1890 he was president of the Red Star Rugby Football Club and became patron of the club two years later. In 1893, he became president of the Tradesmen's Rugby Football Club and vice president of the Wairarapa Rugby Union. Besides all these activities, he was a director of the Wairarapa Caledonian Society and served on the Licensing Bench.

CHAPTER 10

TRIP TO THE OLD COUNTRY

After the death of his father, Augustus decided he would dearly love to see his brothers and sisters again, and their children. He was also keen to visit 'Field Farm' at Nympsfield to see what changes had been made over the last 40 years. Also, Augustus was anxious to show Mary Ann, born in Wellington in 1848, the 'Old Country', particularly the beautiful countryside of the Cotswolds.

Augustus had been deaf since his accident at Abbots Bridge when he was a wagon driver, and he was anxious to see whether any specialist in England could restore his hearing. Also, Mary Ann was starting to suffer from rheumatoid arthritis and Augustus hoped that perhaps a consultant in England could improve her mobility. As an added bonus,

Myer Caselberg.

the Coronation of Edward VII was on the horizon and Augustus and Mary Ann decided it would be very special for them to witness these celebrations in England.

Before they set off on their travels, the ladies in the Masterton district organised an 'At Home' for Mrs Cave at the Foresters Hall. About 50 ladies and a number of gentlemen assembled and there was an extensive programme of musical entertainment – songs by the Misses Cameron, Payton and Cundy and pianoforte solos by the Misses Cope, Meredith, Grey, McKenzie and Cameron. After tea had been taken, Myer Caselberg was called upon to make an address.

Mr Caselberg said he had known both Mr and Mrs Cave for a number of years. Of Mr Cave he needed to say very little. It was commonly said "that Gus Cave's word was as good as his bond." He scarcely knew in what terms of appreciation to refer to Mrs Cave. Everyone spoke of her as always ready to help and assist in any way she could. She was a good neighbour and exemplary in all her relationships. On behalf of the ladies, the pleasing duty devolved upon him to present Mrs Cave with a travelling rug. He hoped, and they all hoped, that when Mrs Cave wrapped it round herself on her travels, she would remember her Masterton friends. He concluded by wishing Mr and Mrs Cave a pleasant voyage, an enjoyable tour, and a safe return. Mr Caselberg's remarks were received with applause.

Duncan McGregor said he did not come there to make a speech, but he would like to say a few words on the occasion of the departure of Mr and Mrs Cave for the 'Old Country'. The presence of such a number of ladies testified to the esteem in which Mrs Cave was held. He had known Mr Cave before that gentleman got married, and he had always been considered a lucky young man through having been fortunate enough to secure such a splendid wife as Mrs Cave. He thought every wife's chief duty and aim in life should be to aid and support her husband, and he was sure Mr Cave would bear him out that Mrs Cave had been all a good helpmate should be. Their old friend was going to accompany his wife to the place where his boyhood had been spent, and he was sure everyone joined in best wishes for their fullest enjoyment of their holiday, and a safe return.

After singing 'Auld Lang Syne', those present said farewell to Mr and Mrs Cave and a very pleasing function was brought to a close.

A short time later some 50 settlers and residents of Masterton, representing the Racing Club, A & P Association, and other local organisations, assembled at Messrs Lowes and Iorns for the purpose of making a presentation to Augustus prior to his departure to the 'Old Country'.

James Macara occupied the chair. He remarked that no doubt they were all cognizant with the object of the present gathering. They had assembled to wish Mr and Mrs Cave a pleasant voyage, an enjoyable trip and a safe return. Mr Macara said that at first, it was intended by the members of the Racing Club to make a small presentation to Mr Cave as a token of their esteem and respect. However, others wished to join in and, as they all could not be entirely excluded, the presentation had developed into one from the Racing Club and other friends. He hoped Mr Cave would thoroughly enjoy his trip, and no doubt, when at Home, he would be thinking of his Masterton friends and associations. They all wished Mr and Mrs Cave a safe journey to the land of his birth. In presenting to Mr Cave an elegant 'companion', with all requisites and suitably inscribed, Mr Macara said that it was a small token of respect and good fellowship from the Masterton Racing Club and other friends. There was great applause.

The 'companion' bore the following inscription: "A W Cave Esq., as a token of respect from the Stewards of the Masterton Racing Club and other friends, on the eve of his departure for England." On its front, in large letters, were the initials "A.W.C."

On rising, Augustus was received with much applause. He stated that owing to his deafness, he had not been able

George Heron.

to hear all that Mr Macara had said about him, but he had known Mr Macara for a long time past, and if he had said anything against him, he had never heard it. There was a great deal of laughter here from the gathering. He felt very proud to see so many friends, including old settlers and town residents. He was also pleased to see so many present with whom he had been associated for years past. The gift was a handsome one, and he appreciated it more than if they had given him £500. He concluded by saying that he hoped to be able to return amongst them, and continue to be good friends. His speech was greeted with much applause.

Fred Hill explained the way the presentation had been arranged. It was originally intended to be from the Racing Club, but outside people expressed their wish to subscribe. Several subscriptions were accepted, but as they were coming in so fast they had to refuse any further donations. However, they had invited all friends to be present. All who were present, Mr Hill was sure, were friends, although only a very small proportion of Mr Cave's many friends were represented. They all joined in wishing Mr and Mrs Cave an enjoyable trip Home and a safe return, and hoped Mr Cave would return invigorated and ready to again enter into public affairs.

Augustus replied by saying that as regards again taking up public work, he did not think he would, owing to his unfortunate deafness. He intended to endeavour to have his hearing restored, if possible, whilst at Home.

The speeches were continued by Mr J A Hives who said that, although he had known Mr Cave a comparatively short time, they were the best of friends. He hoped Mr Cave would not stop at home because it would be a great loss to the district. This was greeted with much applause.

The next speaker was Edwin Meredith who said that as the present was more from the Racing Club, he felt somewhat as an interloper, but all friends having been invited, he would be failing in his duty as a settler and a man if he did not attend to bid Mr Cave bon voyage. Mr Cave was a prominent man in a quiet way. He was one of their best farmers. He had taken the lead, and always helped in every forward work that had been for the advancement of the district. He was one of the best and strongest allies in starting the A. & P. Association. He was also a conspicuous member of the Racing Club as a man who always "ran straight". This was greeted with applause. The same characteristic applied to everything he was connected with. As Mr Cave was a man of observation, when they welcomed him back from his trip, they would find no doubt that he would have picked up many new ideas. Also, he will doubtless be able to give some of the old farmers at home, a few "wrinkles". There was laughter and applause at this statement. He wished Mr and Mrs Cave bon voyage and a safe return.

George Heron then spoke. He said he had known Mr Cave for the past 40 years and went on to say that he could heartily endorse all that had been said by previous speakers. Mr Cave had been a good settler, and a credit to the farming community and to Masterton, as well as to himself. He wished Mr and Mrs Cave a pleasant voyage and safe return.

Mr C A Pownall said he was very pleased to be present, both as a member of the Racing Club and as mayor of Masterton. The town owed a great deal to Mr Cave and other people of his stamp. Undoubtedly, the town owed much to those farmers around, who had, as in Mr Cave's instance, for a number of years done a great deal in employing labour and purchasing goods in the town. A man of his class is very useful to any community. He hoped Mr Cave would return with his hearing improved, and be able to take up public matters again. He had worked with Mr Cave for about 12 years in the Racing Club. They had always got along satisfactorily and amicably, and Mr Cave's name, as president, was a sufficient guarantee of the integrity of the Club. This was greeted with great applause.

Next, Mr E. E. Chamberlain said he believed he had known Mr Cave as long as anyone else present in the room that afternoon. They were old friends on the road, and always stuck together. They always helped one another when getting in difficulties when on the bad roads. He joined with the others in wishing Mr and Mrs Cave a very pleasant trip and hoped they would return greatly improved in health. As far as straightforwardness and honesty were concerned, Mr Cave could not be beaten. This was greeted with much applause.

The final speaker was Walter Perry who remarked that he would like to have seen the A & P Association connected more prominently with the presentation. However, as far as Mr Cave was concerned he was ever willing to give information on farming matters, and had been like a second father to the speaker. Mr Cave had taken a prominent part in many institutions, successfully bringing the A & P Association out of difficulties and acting in a similar capacity for the Racing Club. He wished Mr and

Walter Perry.

Mrs Cave a pleasant trip and a safe return.

In reply Augustus said he had always done his best to further the interests of the A & P Association and Racing Club and would continue to do so. If he came back safely, he would still take the same interest in the two institutions.

The meeting then joined in singing 'He's a Jolly Good Fellow,' and afterwards cheers were given for Augustus and Mary Ann. Before the gathering dispersed, those present took the opportunity to bid Augustus goodbye personally, accompanying the handshaking with hearty wishes for a pleasant trip and safe and speedy return.

I have not been able to find any details of the trip but Augustus and Mary Ann returned to Masterton in January 1903 after a wonderful holiday of over 10 months. Besides witnessing the Coronation celebrations and journeying to Nympsfield in the Cotswolds, they visited various parts of Europe. On their return both stated that they greatly benefited from their holiday and Augustus, who attended the Caledonian Sports Day a short time after their return, was congratulated on having such a splendid trip.

CHAPTER 11

THE RETIREMENT YEARS

After returning from their holiday to the 'Old Country' and Europe, Augustus continued with his interests in the Masterton Agricultural and Pastoral Association and the Masterton Racing Club. He was steward for the A & P Show in February and was again elected president of the Racing Club. In April, he also became president of the Farmers and Commercial Club.

Augustus gradually eased back on his farming activities and on March 28 1907, at the age of 67, he sold the 284 acres named 'Rangitumau Block' to the Shaw brothers for £2,556. This was the land at the end of the road which was named after Augustus and was the property he had purchased nearly 30 years previously for £675 from McRae Drummond.

I have not been able to establish when Augustus and Mary Ann moved permanently to their Masterton town house called 'Nympsfield', but in 1911 the Electoral Roll indicates this house was their main residence. It still stands today and is indeed a fine property. Sadly, 'Woodleigh' farmhouse burned down some time in the past. However, with the

The Caves' town house, 'Nympsfield'.

help of maps, I am fairly confident I have pinpointed its exact location, especially as there is a marvellous old oak tree proudly standing nearby.

'Nympsfield' is situated at the corner of High Street, opposite the Church of the Epiphany, whose annual garden parties the Caves hosted. Their property was very large and extended from Harley Street through to High Street and up to and including what is now South Park. In fact the Caves employed a person full-time to look after the garden and the land. Over the ensuing years much of this land was given away by Augustus and Mary Ann.

Mary Ann's rheumatoid arthritis sadly worsened over the years and photographs show her sitting on a large couch. A succession of relatives acted as nurses and companion helps for Mary Ann, some of them living for a while at 'Nympsfield'. One of these relatives was Florrie Cox, Mary Ann's niece, who is in a photograph with Mary Ann and Augustus in their garden in 1912.

Augustus Cave at 'Nympsfield'.

Margaret Thomas, whose great-grandfather was William Cave, told me a story about Augustus which her sister Edyth had recounted to her. Quite often there were tea parties at 'Nympsfield' because Mary Ann could not go out very much. The ladies attending these tea parties would normally arrive wearing pretty clothes and hats. At this time Edyth was a tiny girl and every time she came with her parents, Augustus would take her hand whilst the ladies were chatting and lead her into the bedroom where all the coats and hats were placed. He then encouraged her to try on all the hats to their shared amusement.

During my research I came across Augustus' birthday book dated 1885. This was a most fascinating discovery as it showed, in chronological order, the various birthdays of all his and his wife's relatives. The book contains the huge total of 65 birthdays and includes the names of the various branches of the family.

At 'Nympsfield': Sarah Cox, Phebe Johnston, Mary Ann Cave and Augustus Cave.

Of great interest to me, was the entry for my grandmother Kate Insall and her twin sister Alice on December 15th. Her mother was Mary Elizabeth Cave, Augustus' sister who had married John Insall on August 16 1864. There were also another 13 entries of various members of the Insall family. Augustus had two other sisters, Charlotte and Sarah, who had both married into the Hewett family, and there were several birthday dates for this branch of the family.

Mary Ann's mother, Sarah Bourton, was first married to Richard Iorns and later, after his death, to Henry Bannister and there are many Bannister names in the book and an entry for Sarah Cox née Iorns. Sarah Bourton had a younger sister Mary who married into the Perry family, another of the famous pioneer families of the Wairarapa and there is an entry under January 3 for L Perry. Even the mayor of Masterton, C A Pownall, is mentioned in the book under July 8.

Further evidence of a large family was Augustus' will, made on December 6 1917, which included legacies to many members of the Cave, Bannister and Iorns families

– in total there are 20 substantial legacies to these relatives or, on their death, to their various children.

Finally, on March 29 1919, Augustus sold all his remaining farmland to Frank Ratcliffe for £20,562. This included 365 acres in the 'Te Ahitainga Block' and 222 acres in the 'Taueru Section'. At the end of 1919 he fell ill with liver problems and died four months later on Sunday, April 4 1920, at the age of 80. Despite her infirmities, Mary Ann, 72 years old at this time, lived another 13 years. She died on September 9 1933.

There were several obituaries written about Augustus, but in my opinion the one following, published in the *Wairarapa Daily Times*, most completely summed up the man and his life:

The late Mr Cave

"In the death of Mr A W Cave, Masterton has lost a pioneer settler whose name was revered from one end of the district to the other.

As a farmer he was most industrious and painstaking; as a neighbour he was incomparable; as a sportsman he was honest and straightforward, and always 'played the game'; and as a friend he was the embodiment of fidelity. Genial in disposition, ever ready to help those who were in need, as straight as an arrow in all his dealings, he was indeed and in truth one of nature's gentlemen. Few men in the district have enjoyed the popularity of the late Mr Cave, and had it not been for a physical infirmity, he could have attained the very highest position at the command of the people. His name will always be associated with the most honoured and respected of our pioneer settlers, and his passing will leave a void in the community which will be difficult to fill. By his sterling character he endeared himself to all, and he has ended in peace a career of usefulness that will be indelibly inscribed upon the pages of Wairarapa history."

CHAPTER 12

VISCOUNT CAVE OF RICHMOND

I sent a draft copy of my manuscript to Bob Russell to show him the great success of my researches in New Zealand. After reading it, he suggested a meeting since, with the increasingly widespread use of the Internet, it was possible he could discover new information for my family trcc. Bob duly came down to Devon for a weekend and we spent many interesting hours on the computer filling in more gaps regarding my ancestors.

Bob had become a real expert on genealogy and it was fascinating watching him surf the various websites and gaining information on my ancestry practically every time he entered a new site. He 'Googled' the name 'Cave' and soon discovered there was a Cave Society devoted to family history and they produced a magazine called *Caveman*. He managed to access the October 2001 issue where we were excited to discover: "Lord George Cave, Lord Chancellor in the 1920s, was descended from the Caves of Owlpen".

While my great-great-grandfather, William Cave, came from Nympsfield, his grandfather, Thomas Cave, was born in the nearby tiny village of Owlpen. We spent the next few hours busily trying to prove a connection between my ancestors and those of Lord Cave. At 1.30am we finally had the proof.

My great-great-great-great-grandfather, Thomas Cave, born in 1722, married Sarah Gingell in 1750. I am descended from one son, Thomas Cave; they also had another son, John, who married Hannah Holder in 1777. They, in turn, had a son, George, who married Harriet Gould in 1815 and one of their sons, Thomas, was Lord Cave's father. I was astonished to think I had another illustrious ancestor. It was also extraordinary that two such illustrious men – Augustus William Cave and Lord George Cave – should come from such a tiny village in the Cotswolds.

On that Sunday evening I telephoned Hugh Cave, the

secretary of the Cave Society, who was most helpful. He was very interested to learn of my researches in New Zealand as the society was not aware of this Cave connection. A few days later he sent me numerous family trees which confirmed I was indeed related to Lord Cave. He also told me about a very good book written about him, *Lord Cave – A Memoir,* by Sir Charles Mallet and published by John Murray in 1931.

The next day I visited my great friend Ross Greig who acts as my e-mail letterbox. He typed in 'Lord Chancellor' on a certain website and up came a list of all the people who had held the post since 1068. There were certainly some interesting names including Thomas A Becket in 1154, Cardinal Wolsley in 1515 and Sir Thomas More in 1529. Another holder of this post, in 1970, was Quintin Hogg who, incidentally, had presented me with a prize when I was at Bristol Grammar School 18 years earlier. We also ordered the Lord Cave book on line from, of all places, Springfield, Illinois, USA.

Viscount Cave in the robes of Lord Chancellor of Great Britain.

Later in the week I visited the reference library in Plymouth and looked up Lord Cave in *Who Was Who 1916-1928* and in *The Concise Dictionary of National Biography.* This produced some fascinating information. He was born in London in 1856 and educated at the Merchant Taylors' School and St. John's College, Oxford. After being called to the bar in 1880, he practised as a barrister for a number of years, becoming King's Counsel and Recorder of Guildford in 1904. Two years later, he was elected Conservative member of parliament for the Kingston Division of Surrey and was appointed a member of the Royal Commission on Land Purchase in 1908.

He served as Standing Counsel to Oxford University for two years, was Attorney General to the Prince of Wales and was appointed Solicitor General and knighted in 1915. Then, in 1916, he became Home Secretary in Lloyd George's coalition government, holding the post for three years.

In 1918, he was ennobled as Viscount Cave of Richmond, Surrey and the following year he became a Lord of Appeal and chaired a number of commissions, including one concerned with Southern Rhodesia. In 1922, he became Lord Chancellor in Bonar Law's government and then served in this capacity again in Baldwin's first administration.

Then, I was particularly pleased to note, because of my Oxford connections with Wadham, St Edmund Hall and Jesus Colleges, he was elected Chancellor of Oxford University in 1925. In 1921 he was made a GCMG – Knight Grand Cross of the Order of St. Michael and St. George. He died in 1928 aged 72.

What a wonderful and interesting life Lord Cave had led with a long list of impressive achievements. It must have been very difficult and demanding to have been Home Secretary during the First World War

One news item that particularly caught my eye was that in 1927 he adjudicated the rival claims of Canada and Newfoundland regarding Labrador. He must have possessed great mediation skills to be asked to sort out this difficult problem and it seemed to answer a question about Augustus William Cave that had puzzled me for some time.

Why had the local Maori presented Augustus with such an impressive waistcoat? According to Mrs. Rewi at Te Papa in Wellington, this sort of gift was very rarely given. Gareth Winter had surmised it was given because Augustus, highly respected by both Maori and the local council, had mediated between them over various contentious matters. Having read about Lord Cave's involvement with Labrador, I am now inclined to agree with Gareth's supposition.

I later discovered Lord Cave was awarded the GCMG because, in 1919, he led a commission to South Africa to decide on the appropriate compensation to be awarded to the British South Africa Company for the loss of their investment in Southern Rhodesia.

The Lord Cave book duly arrived from America and I was not surprised, given his long and distinguished career, that it extended to 328 pages. I used to live in Bladon, near Woodstock in Oxfordshire where Blenheim Palace is situated and where Sir Winston Churchill was born and laid to rest. I had hoped Lord Cave might have come into direct contact with Sir Winston and I was very pleased to see, on page 135, that Winston Churchill had appointed Cave to hold an inquiry into the conduct of the police.

I could also take considerable pride in Stanley Baldwin's letter to Lord Cave on March 28 1928 which included:

> "The King was anxious to confer some special recognition on you at this moment, and I know you will forgive me for anticipating what would have been yours at the end of the Parliament, and advising him that an earldom should be given you on resignation. He gladly and immediately assented.
>
> "You must not worry about anything, but stand firm in the knowledge of the confidence and affection which every one of your colleagues has for you."

Sadly, Lord Cave died the very next day, the day it was announced he would be created an earl. In the event, his widow was created Countess Cave of Richmond. They had one child who died at birth and so the viscountcy ceased with his death, and the earldom when his wife died in 1938.

There was a parallel here with Augustus William Cave whose only child died when just six years old.

I also discovered there are several oil portraits of Lord Cave by various artists.

To date, I have been to the Inner Temple and seen the 1925 painting by R G Eves; to St. John's College, Oxford where Francis Dodd's portrait hangs proudly in the minstrels' gallery above the dining hall, and to the House of Lords to see Aidan Savage's painting in the Speaker's residence. I then commissioned a professional photographer, Mike Fear, to photograph all three paintings which he has transferred on to canvas. They look just like

Viscount Cave as Chancellor of Oxford University.

the originals. I now have all three proudly hanging in my home. I have yet to see other portraits at Merchant Taylors' School and County Hall, Kingston-upon-Thames. I am also getting a 'reader's ticket' for the House of Commons so I can look up his speeches in Hansard. I am sure the further investigation of Lord Cave's life will give me much pleasure and enjoyment.

Sir Charles Mallet's book about Lord Cave ended with this:

The Cave family crest on a plaque at Richmond Palace. © Peter Denton.

"And he earned more. He earned through life the reputation of a colleague and opponent whom everyone could trust. He never shirked a duty. He never failed a friend. He went on his way, with a certain stately simplicity of nature, doing to the best of his ability, single-heartedly and singularly well, every task fate set before him. He won the best of all the gifts of fortune, a full measure of affection and esteem. And in his title to that great possession no one who knew him will refuse to acquiesce."

I was immediately struck by the similarity of these fine words to Augustus' obituary quoted at the end of the last chapter. Both men were straightforward and honest in all their dealings and, because of this, they both enjoyed great respect and affection from the people with whom they came into contact.

During their 2005 European tour my relatives, Andrea and Tom Wyeth from Masterton, came to Plymouth to visit us. While walking in the Barbican, a very old part of Plymouth from where the Pilgrim Fathers set sail for America, we found a small shop specialising in genealogy. In the course of conversation, family crests were mentioned and, after telling the owner of the shop of my researches, he suggested he could look up the family name. It was a complete surprise to learn that the Caves did indeed have a family crest.

When I returned home that afternoon, I immediately rang the College of Arms and they confirmed the find. The family motto was 'Cave Deus Videt' or 'Beware God Sees'.

When I went to the Varsity Soccer Match at Fulham football club in 2006, I met Lord Faulkner of Worcester who very kindly offered to show me my family's coat of arms and the portrait of Lord Cave, as Lord Chancellor, in the River Room. My wife, Kathy, and I spent a very pleasant afternoon at the House of Lords looking at both the coat of arms and the painting. We were also entertained to a lovely tea in the sumptuous dining room - it was rather a shock to see my family displayed in such magnificent surroundings!

Recently I discovered my family's crest is also displayed as a plaque on the walls of Richmond Palace, a royal palace from 1327 to 1649. George Cave lived at Wardrobe Court, formerly The Wardrobe of Henry VIII, for 38 years. The plaque states that George Cave of Richmond GCMG was Lord Chancellor of Great Britain and Chancellor of Oxford University. Our crest is at the top and the plaque also displays our family motto – *Cave Deus Videt.*

Viscount Cave was granted a Knight Grand Cross of the Most Distinguished Order of Saint Michael and Saint George on February 1 1921. This order have their own chapel in St. Paul's with stalls and members' banners displayed from the ceiling and every year there is a special service in the cathedral followed by a reception. In 2007 we went to this service and to the reception in the crypt which we found very interesting. The award is given to ambassadors and we found the members and their wives very friendly.

The 2008 service was special because the monarch attends every eighth year. The very lavish reception was held the night before at the Foreign and Commonwealth Office. The service the next morning at St. Paul's was spectacular. Senior members of the Order dressed in their robes and displayed their banners paraded, with the Queen, in a very long procession, before and after the service.

I wonder what other wonderful surprises await me if I have the time to investigate all the other branches of my family. For instance, the Flemings on the maternal side of my family were basket makers. I do know some of them emigrated to Sherborne near Boston, USA during the 19th century.

CHAPTER 13

THE GIFT OF A BELL
TO MAORI

As noted earlier, Augustus purchased land on two occasions from the Maori chief Wi Tinitara Te Kaewa. Augustus later employed the chief's son, Rimene Witinitara, on his farm.

As Augustus' farm was not far from the Te Ore Ore marae, it is very likely he would have provided food, such as sheep, when the local Maori had a feast at their meeting house. However, I feel the link between Augustus and the local Maori went a lot deeper than this. Augustus was clearly a very well respected member of the local community and pillar of society locally. According to Gareth Winter of the Wairarapa Archive, because of his many connections with so many associations, Augustus was used as a mediator by the local Maori and the local authorities if any dispute needed to be settled between them. Augustus developed a reputation for being straight as an arrow in all his dealings and I am sure both sides trusted him and felt he would mediate in a dispute in the fairest way possible.

One can only surmise whether it was because of his skills in mediation, or because he had paid a fair price for Maori land, or because he employed Maori on his farm and he treated them fairly, but the local Maori bestowed on Augustus a very rare honour. They took considerable time and trouble to make him a woven flax waistcoat, which he doubtless wore with great honour and pride when he attended any functions at the Te Ore Ore marae. In New Zealand I enquired from a large auctioneering firm, which specialises in selling Maori and historical artifacts, about the waistcoat; they informed me that in all their years of trading they had only heard of one other waistcoat ever being made for a pakeha (European). This was an extraordinary revelation and I feel extremely proud of this strong tie between Augustus and the local Maori community.

After my first visit to Masterton, the waistcoat was loaned by Barbara Nichols to the Museum of New Zealand, Te Papa Tongarewa, in Wellington. Betty Rewi, the collection manager in the Maori Art & History Department at Te Papa described the waistcoat as follows: "The long blade of the New Zealand flax has been evenly stripped and then boiled, gentian violet was used to dye some of the strips and then interwoven creating this effective pattern. A fashion statement before its time, the back is of grey cotton with a cream cotton underlay." She also said: "It is a valuable and significant treasure", and in a further letter to me on May 16 2003 she wrote "that the waistcoat is the guardian of your history in New Zealand and has extended itself to England to gather you into the historical richness is so very remarkable."

After five years, the waistcoat was returned to Masterton and in December 2003 it was given by Barbara Nichols to Aratoi, the local museum, together with a woven kete (bag). On receiving the two items, Rangitane o Wairarapa cultural adviser Mike Kawana said: "I was first of all thanking Barbara for bringing the two taonga to Aratoi; then I paid my respects to the people who made the taonga."

During my researches it became very clear that the Maori of Te Ore Ore held both my great-great-grandfather William Cave and his son Augustus in very great regard. They had honoured Augustus with the making of the waistcoat, an extremely rare object, and the laying of the korowai (cloak) over William's coffin as it was lowered into the ground was quite extraordinary.

I am extremely proud of this connection with the local Maori and I felt that if it was humanly possible, I would like to do something for them.

During Andrea and Tom Wyeth's stay with us in England in 2006 Tom mentioned a friend, Pani Himona, who was on the committee of the Te Ore Ore marae, and promised to contact him on his return to discuss the possibility of a suitable gift or koha. This suggestion certainly produced results. The marae committee met and identified the lack of a bell to call the people to prayer (karakia), to meals or to meetings (hui).

When this proposal of a gift of a bell was suggested to

me, I was enthusiastic and immediately offered to fund the whole project. I could instantly see what an appropriate gift this would be – as well as being of great use to the marae, a bell would be a constant reminder of the link between Augustus and his Maori friends.

However, finding a suitably large bell proved very difficult for the committee. A distributor said one would be extremely hard to find and would cost in the region of $1200 – $1400. Considerable time was spent looking for a bell in various shops and following up leads about where one might be located. But, as has been the case throughout this incredible journey of mine, there was another extraordinary occurrence. Cyril McEwen, the last surviving member of the Wainuiomata branch of the Ex-Naval Seamen's Association, heard of the committee's problem. The branch was now defunct, but he had its bell and considered the Te Ore Ore marae project would be a very appropriate home for this taonga (treasured object). I gather the committee was extremely grateful to Mr McEwen, particularly since the bell already had a history of its own.

It was now necessary to erect a bell tower. Another extraordinary thing happened. Pani Himona's son, Peter, is a Maori carver of excellent reputation and he immediately

Coming onto the marae with the bell in foreground. Courtesy Wairarapa News.

offered to do the carvings on the bell tower free of charge. The committee gratefully accepted his most generous offer and the project began to take shape. He constructed the bell tower from totara timber left over from the Nga Tau e Waru Carvings Restoration Project completed in April 2004. On my behalf, Tom Wyeth paid for the paint and other materials used during construction. I was pleased that I was at least able to make more of a contribution than simply canvassing the idea of a gift for the Te Ore Ore Maori.

The carved bell structure was completed by Peter, and was blessed while an educational gathering (wananga) was being held at the marae. Tom Wyeth sent me photographs of the bell tower and bell and it looked very fine and imposing. All that was needed was for me to come to Masterton to see the finished product. I organised our fourth world trip for the months of January-March 2008 and a date was set by the Te Ore Ore Maori committee for the welcome (powhiri) on Sunday, February 10 2008. I gathered it was to be a social and historical occasion, including lunch for my party and Cyril McEwen and his wife. An e-mail from Pani Himona to Tom Wyeth said he hoped the ceremony would be "a memorable time for our benefactors".

I asked to the ceremony the people who had particularly helped me in my Augustus and William Cave researches – Gareth Winter, Masterton archivist whose help and guidance had been so useful over the past 12 years, and his wife; my relative Margaret Thomas and her friend, Barbara Nichols, who had produced the illustrious waistcoat back in 1996. Also I invited Beryl Stuart who is related to me by marriage, her son Cameron, daughter Andrea and son-in-law Tom Wyeth. I also asked Glenys Hansen, whom we had stayed with on two occasions and

Arriving at the meeting house. Courtesy Wairarapa News.

Christopher Pope entering the meeting house. Courtesy Wairarapa News.

had done much typing and research for me. Luckily our friends, Nonnie and Alan Duncan from England, were going to be in Masterton at the same time which was pleasing as they had helped and supported us on numerous occasions in the past.

Sunday February 10 2008 soon arrived and despite a poorish weather forecast, it was a hot and sunny morning. We were asked to be at the marae at 11.00 am sharp and, on our arrival, I was glad to see everybody I had asked was there and on time. Margaret Thomas brought her granddaughter and so there were, including Mr. and Mrs. McEwen, 16 of us as visitors. We were joined by a female elder (kuia) Angie Pourau, who had a moko chin tattoo and a male elder (kaumatua) named Nelson Rangi. It was very appropriate that he should be joining the visitors (manuhiri) as he was descended from Joseph Iorns, brother of Polly, Augustus Cave's wife.

At 11.00am we advanced to the centre of the courtyard, indicating our readiness to be called (karanga) onto the marae by the female elder, Hinerau Te Tau, of the local inhabitants (tangata whenua). She commenced the karanga in Maori and Angie Pourau responded in Maori on our behalf as we advanced. I gathered afterwards that she had said: "We are coming in peace and we are coming to pay our respects". Protocol demanded the short walk to the meeting house be halted about halfway to give both tangata whenua and manuhiri an opportunity to remember those who had passed away and to grieve over them. As we stopped, I thought how appropriate it was for us to be thinking of our ancestors as that was the reason I had come to New Zealand in the first place.

Given the day's heat, the Te Ore Ore committee had decided to have the welcome (powhiri) inside the meeting house (tipuna whare) which was named 'Nga Tau e Waru' (the eight years). When we reached the meeting house we removed our shoes, then went inside and sat down on the seats provided, with the menfolk sitting in the front as protocol demanded. The tangata whenua sat opposite us.

The welcome speech (whaikorero) was made in Maori by Bill Wright and was followed by a song (waiata). Nelson Rangi responded in Maori on our behalf. He paid homage to the ancestors of the Maori and to our ancestors. The Maori have a stronger concept of their ancestors being with them than we do. A further song was sung and finally Angie Pourau recited a prayer (karakia). Pani Himona then invited us to cross to the paepae (front bench) to hongi (pressing of noses in greeting). This we all did, the hongi ending the formal part of the ceremonial welcome.

Next, the chairs were arranged in a very large circle with me wondering what was going to happen. In fact, we had a greeting (mihi). Everybody was invited to sit down in no particular order and then one of the tangata whenua got to his feet and explained in English who he was, where he came from – namely his river, his mountain, his land – and why he was at the ceremony that day. After he sat down, the person on his right got up and did the same thing. There were about 35 people in the circle and everybody participated. Every person tried to find links with the other people present. It was extraordinary, with some people discovering their ancestors were on the same ship that sank near Wellington. Bill Wright had Scottish ancestors as did our friend Alan Duncan. The general idea of a mihi was to make everyone feel comfortable and the atmosphere was certainly very cordial and relaxed. Gareth Winter even told an amusing story about a Sister from St. Bride's Convent and the Pope.

When it came to Peter Himona's turn, he suggested we all go outside to the bell tower so he could explain exactly what each carving represented. He said much thought had been given before he commenced carving and he hoped he had conveyed in the carving the meaning of life. He said the name of the carved bell structure was 'Ka Puta mai Tatou' and it told the story of the birth of the people of this marae.

> "Ka Puta mai Tatou' starts at the beginning of time. Light enters into the world as Rangi and Papa are separated. A painted spiral represents light coming into the world, with the first figure, directly above the first pou (support), symbolic of

the separation of Rangi and Papa. A similar figure is above the second pou. A manaia, an abstract carved figure, follows. Manaia on the crossbeam represents our guardians who protect, teach, and care for us. Manaia surround us and the bell. We are the human-like forms on the crossbeam. A bell has been carved on the crossbeam so that the bell gifted to us is acknowledged when it is removed for storage. The placing of the legs of the figures represents the movement of time. The placing of hands on our shoulders is a sign of caring and the transfer of knowledge from our guardians and tipuna (ancestors). The continuation of the spiral and light across the crossbeam binds the crossbeam carvings together. A stake is handed to us that we use to mark our ground. This action acknowledges our marae as our kainga tuturu.

"There are two pou, each with a carved figure. One figure is placed higher than the other representing the descending of generations from one to another. The placement of these figures is such that if there was another pou, the figure on that pou would be placed on the marae, meaning it is our time now. The carvings on the crossbeam and the placement of the figures on the pou are designed to move your thoughts from left to right, onto the marae. The figures on each pou represent tipuna who have gone before us. For everyone visiting the marae, these figures will represent their own tipuna of bygone days. The two pou are not heavily carved with surface decorations so their shape or form is admired rather than their surface decorations. The placement of hands on one pou, one above the other, rather than next to each other, is a sign of contentedness.

"'Ka Puta mai Tatou' is an earthy red colour representative of Papatuanuku, our mother earth."

After everyone had spoken, Pani Himona said a few words and then I was invited to make a short speech. I stressed how proud I was of my family's connection with Maori and the Te Ore Ore marae. I told the assembled gathering about Augustus' cousin Viscount Cave and how excited I was to learn he had become Lord Chancellor of Great Britain on two occasions, Home Secretary during the First World War, Chancellor of the University of Oxford and was awarded the GCMG. This last appointment is the sixth most senior order, the Knight Grand Cross of the Order of St. Michael and St. George. However, I then stressed that I was just as proud of Augustus's achievements in Masterton as I was of Viscount Cave's rise to fame in England.

I then went on to say that if one of my ancestors had not added a plaque on the family box tomb in Nympsfield churchyard recording that my great-great-grandfather had died at 'Woodleigh', Masterton, I would not have been standing there that day, for none of my family knew of this New Zealand connection.

> "It has been an incredible journey with many twists and turns and I have discovered so much information about William Cave and his son Augustus and the early history of Masterton. At times I have felt as if someone has been guiding me along the way. There was the instance when I went back to the Information Centre to thank them for their help. I picked out the lady I thought was in charge and discovered she had been ill for some time and this was her first day back at work. She asked me the name of my relative and she told me she had gone to school with a Margaret Cave, who

The bell and its intricately carved tower. Courtesy Wairarapa News.

had since married a Mr. Thomas. I met Margaret, the waistcoat made by your ancestors was produced and I discovered Augustus' connection with the Te Ore Ore marae."

I said I was so lucky to have met people who actually knew something personal about Augustus and his life. For instance, Jim Rimene had told me in 2003 that his grandfather was the only person who could ride one of Augustus' stallions, information that had obviously been passed down though the generations by word of mouth.

I ended my speech by saying my wife, Kathy, and I were very pleased to be able to give something useful back to those whose ancestors had honoured and respected my ancestors in such a wonderful way.

Next, our koha (gift), which was in a sealed white envelope, was placed slowly by me on the ground in front of the elders. One of the elders very slowly picked up our koha and Angie Pourau uttered a prayer of thanks for our gift. Finally, Hinerau Te Tau said a prayer to close proceedings.

A delicious buffet lunch was laid out on a long table at the end of the meeting house and we were told to help ourselves. I was very pleased to see paua fritters on one of the plates. This is a local shellfish delicacy which the Maori have a customary right to collect. We had, in fact, seen many empty paua shells at Castlepoint beach where we had visited with Tom and Andrea a few days earlier. Everyone in our party said how much they had enjoyed the visit to the marae. Kathy and I certainly did and it was, indeed, a red letter day.

Our outward flight to Hong Kong had been a 13 hour trip and we were not all that comfortable during the journey, despite upgrading our tickets to the premium class. Time seemed to pass so slowly and after about five hours into the flight, we even began to wonder whether it was going to be worth making all this effort to go to New Zealand once again. However, after the ceremony we were so glad we had come because the formal proceedings on the marae, in the Maori language, and the mihi afterwards were experiences of a lifetime. We felt very privileged to be part of the powhiri – to have experienced the warmth of the Maori welcome with all its wonderful culture was something special, and to participate in something belonging to another race and culture.

I felt with my gift I had in some small way repaid all the honours the local Maori had bestowed on my ancestors. The story of the friendship and respect between the Maori of Te Ore Ore and my family had gone full circle and I felt very privileged to be part of this story. I have given to the Maori something they tell me will be of great use to them. Pani Himona said the bell is a living thing and, every time it is rung, it will remind them of their ancestors and my ancestors and the close bond that existed between them. Angie Pourau, one of the elders (kuia) came up to me during lunch and said, "You and Kathy will always be most welcome here at the marae". We felt very honoured and so lucky to have had this precious experience.

It was wonderful to know that my ancestors, Augustus and his father William, would have also enjoyed the Maori welcome and culture over a hundred years ago at the Te Ore Ore marae.

POSTSCRIPT

As I stated in the Preface, I do hope readers have enjoyed this remarkable story and will now embark on their own journeys to trace ancestors. I cannot guarantee the outcome will be as rewarding as mine but I am sure you will have great fun and satisfaction uncovering the mysteries of your past and I am equally sure you will have some marvellous eureka moments along the way.

During the rest of our travels in New Zealand we talked about the gifts of the waistcoat and the bell to many people and, invariably, they remarked what an interesting and amazing story it was. Kathy and I were made to feel like celebrities and we certainly did not want to leave the country. Consequently, New Zealand has become our second home and its people are very dear to us. Goodness knows who we will support if England play the All Blacks in the 2011 Rugby World Cup final to be held in New Zealand!

BIBLIOGRAPHY

During my research, these books and newspapers have been of great assistance.

Charles Bannister, *Early History of the Wairarapa*, Christchurch, 1999.

A G Bagnall, *Masterton's First Hundred Years*, Masterton, 1954.

Alan Bebbington, *A History of Uley, Gloucestershire*, Uley, 2003.

Ian F Grant, *North of the Waingawa*, Masterton, 1995.

Sir Charles Mallet, *Lord Cave, A Memoir*, London, 1951.

Angus McCallum, *A meeting of gentlemen on matters agricultural: the Masterton Show 1871-1986*, Masterton, 1986.

T A Ryder, *Gloucestershire Through the Ages*, Liverpool, 1950.

Gareth Winter, *The Look of Masterton*, Masterton, 2004.

Wairarapa Daily Times

THE CAVE FAMILY

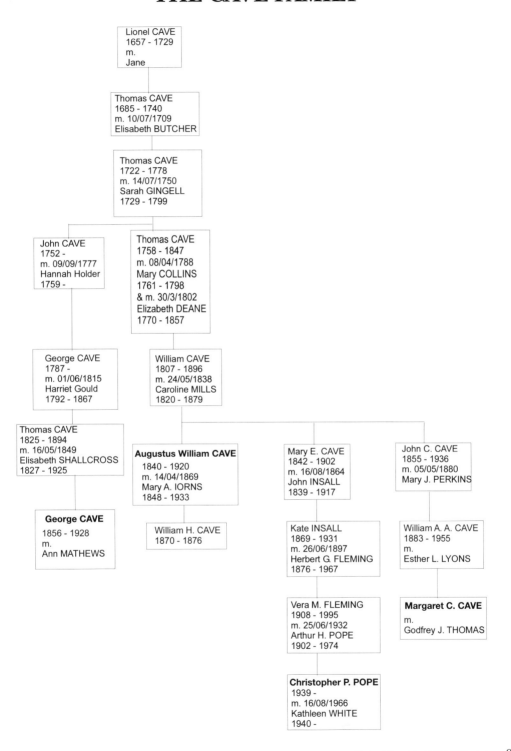

Lionel CAVE
1657 - 1729
m.
Jane

Thomas CAVE
1685 - 1740
m. 10/07/1709
Elisabeth BUTCHER

Thomas CAVE
1722 - 1778
m. 14/07/1750
Sarah GINGELL
1729 - 1799

John CAVE
1752 -
m. 09/09/1777
Hannah Holder
1759 -

Thomas CAVE
1758 - 1847
m. 08/04/1788
Mary COLLINS
1761 - 1798
& m. 30/3/1802
Elizabeth DEANE
1770 - 1857

George CAVE
1787 -
m. 01/06/1815
Harriet Gould
1792 - 1867

William CAVE
1807 - 1896
m. 24/05/1838
Caroline MILLS
1820 - 1879

Thomas CAVE
1825 - 1894
m. 16/05/1849
Elisabeth SHALLCROSS
1827 - 1925

Augustus William CAVE
1840 - 1920
m. 14/04/1869
Mary A. IORNS
1848 - 1933

Mary E. CAVE
1842 - 1902
m. 16/08/1864
John INSALL
1839 - 1917

John C. CAVE
1855 - 1936
m. 05/05/1880
Mary J. PERKINS

George CAVE
1856 - 1928
m.
Ann MATHEWS

William H. CAVE
1870 - 1876

Kate INSALL
1869 - 1931
m. 26/06/1897
Herbert G. FLEMING
1876 - 1967

William A. A. CAVE
1883 - 1955
m.
Esther L. LYONS

Vera M. FLEMING
1908 - 1995
m. 25/06/1932
Arthur H. POPE
1902 - 1974

Margaret C. CAVE
m.
Godfrey J. THOMAS

Christopher P. POPE
1939 -
m. 16/08/1966
Kathleen WHITE
1940 -

THE MASTERS FAMILY

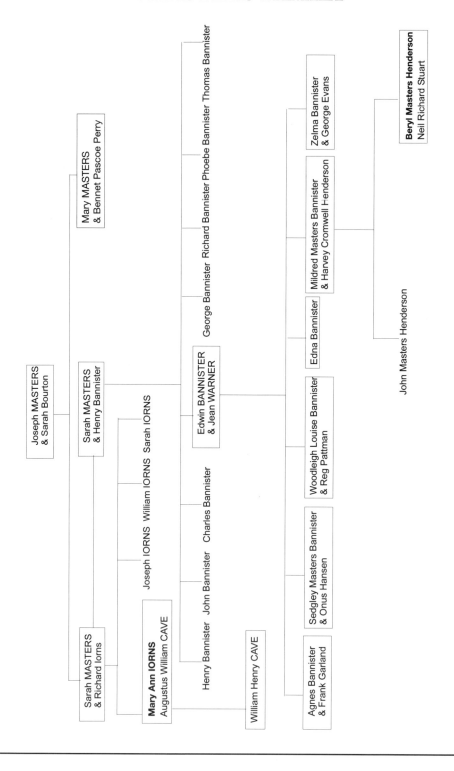

INDEX